Grouse Shooting

Other titles by David Hudson published by Quiller

Shooting Man's Dog
The Working Labrador
The Small Shoot
Working Pointers and Setters
Pheasant Shooting
Gamekeeping
Running your own Shoot

David Hudson

Grouse Shooting

Quiller

Copyright © 2008 David Hudson

First published in the UK in 2008
by Quiller, an imprint of Quiller Publishing Ltd

British Library Cataloguing-in-Publication Data
A catalogue record for this book
is available from the British Library

ISBN 978 1 84689 023 9

Printed in China

Quiller

An imprint of Quiller Publishing Ltd
Wykey House, Wykey, Shrewsbury, SY4 1JA
Tel: 01939 261616 Fax: 01939 261606
E-mail: info@quillerbooks.com
Website: www.countrybooksdirect.com

Contents

Acknowledgements

I owe a very big vote of thanks to a number of people who willingly took time and made the effort to help and advise me with writing this book and in particular allowing me to take photographs of them working and shooting on moors across England and Scotland. Their efforts were much appreciated and I am grateful for their patience and good humour at those times when I and my camera may have been over intrusive. They include: Jeremy Case who has invited Georgina and me to bring our pointers and setters shooting for many years, Colin Organ who drove the tractor and wielded the broom for the heather burning pictures, and James, Pippa and Daphne Scott-Harden who allowed me to photograph two wonderful days shooting on their beautiful moor. Ian and Pauline Withey shared several days grouse counting with us for which thanks are also due to Ben Weatherall and his keepers. Richard MacNicol, Jon Kean, Wilson Young, Julie Organ, Betty Town, Billy Darragh, and many others from the pointer and setter field trial circuit provided sound advice and never complained at being photographed at every turn.

To them, and to everyone else who has contributed, knowingly or not, to the production of this book, a very sincere thank you.

Introduction

I grew up in a small Suffolk village where shooting was almost a way of life. Pheasants and partridges were commonplace, mallard, pigeon, snipe, woodcock, hares and rabbits abounded in the fields, woods and hedgerows. I was given my first air rifle at about nine years of age, bought my first shotgun when I was thirteen and spent many happy hours prowling about the estate on those parts where I was permitted to go with a gun in search of the pigeons and rabbits. Pheasants and partridges were reserved for the landowner and his guests and strictly off limits for everyone else including a small boy with a converted Lee-Enfield rifle firing four-ten cartridges. Even so, I harboured the ambition that one day, albeit long in the future, I might be in a position where I too could stand at a peg and shoot driven partridges and pheasants, but as for grouse… I don't believe that the thought of shooting grouse, much less any hope that I might one day do so ever entered my head. Grouse shooting was, as I understood it, something that was available only to those who were both very rich and very well connected.

I was an avid reader of the *Shooting Times* and whatever books on shooting I could buy or borrow from the local library so I had a reasonable theoretical understanding of grouse and grouse shooting. I also harboured a passionate desire to be involved in anything and everything to do with sporting shooting. Even so, I did not shoot my first grouse until I was around thirty-seven or thirty-eight. Indeed, I must have been in my late twenties before I even saw a grouse alive and in the wild.

It was in Derbyshire on the Duke of Devonshire's Chatsworth Estate where I was watching a Pointer and Setter Field Trial. I had rather more than a passing interest in the stake because my wife,

An English setter on point during a field trial.

The wide open horizons of heather moorland.

Georgina, was running a pointer named Anouska in the trial. Far beyond the thrill of watching one of our dogs competing in a field trial though there was the feeling of exceptional good fortune – of privilege even – at being out on the moor and seeing the undisputed king (or queen for the politically correct) of game birds in its natural environment and actually taking part (albeit vicariously) in the trial. Georgina and Anouska didn't win the trial, though I believe they were awarded a certificate of merit, but that day opened up a whole new world of sport to me.

It wasn't just the sight of the grouse bursting from the heather in front of the pointers and setters, the sound of the cock bird calling 'Go back, go back' as he glided across the heather, nor the elation or despair of the competitors as their dogs completed their run in triumph or disaster. It was the wide open horizons of the moorland; the honeyed scent of the heather; the taste of peat dust on my lips and the feel of rock under my boots; the faint odour of gunpowder as a shot was fired to salute each rising covey and the sheer athleticism of the dogs as they quartered effortlessly over the ground. These wide open spaces were so different from the quiet fields and sleepy woods of my native

Suffolk. No hedgerows or fences. No grassy meadows, no barley, no sugar beet. Rushing burns that babbled their way down the hillside, tumbling over rocks and swirling through dark pools instead of the muddy, placid rivers that wound their way slowly and silently through the water meadows of my home village. A horizon that stretched for miles without a house, a barn, or any other man-made structure in sight apart from stone grouse butts stretching in line across the heather.

There was the sense that this was a wild, natural landscape: one that had not been sculpted by man and for man, but one that remained as nature had made it. (I have since learned that grouse moorland, in common with virtually every other type of landscape in Britain, is almost entirely a product of man's interference with nature, but nevertheless, it did – and does – feel wild in a way that arable land can never do.) A heather moor on a fine day can lift the spirits and gladden the heart of the gloomiest of souls. (It is also fair to say that the same heather moor, when swept by a cold rain driven before a gale of wind on a dark November afternoon will feel somewhat less welcoming and uplifting.) But leaving such matters of detail aside, on that distant July day I understood instinctively, more completely than any amount of books and magazines could ever have informed me, just what it was that made grouse shooting such an attractive proposition.

The grouse is a handsome bird certainly, if you are ever fortunate enough to get a clear view of one, but in purely aesthetic terms they can hardly be said to be better looking

The sheer joy of grouse shooting is plain to see in this Gun's face.

than a grey partridge or that bird's slightly more gaudy French cousin. A cock pheasant pitted against a grouse in a beauty contest would surely win hands down unless the judges were inclined to disqualify the pheasant on the grounds of over-flamboyance. Grouse, whether they are driven to you or walked up by you, may certainly offer superb sport that can test the best of shots, but the same can be said of partridges bursting over a hedgerow; a high pheasant curling across the wind; a woodcock flitting through birch woods or even a pigeon skimming over the trees on a February roost shoot. And on the table, though a young grouse, lightly roasted, is a meal fit for the most discerning palate the same can be said for a partridge, a pheasant or – once again – a plump pigeon.

Yet sportsmen from all parts of the globe who gather in Scotland and the north of England every August and pay enormous amounts of money to shoot grouse will tell you, unhesitatingly, that the red grouse provides the finest sporting shooting available anywhere in the world. Why should this be so?

I would suggest there are a number of reasons that, taken together, explain the popularity of grouse shooting. For a start, the red grouse is found only in the British Isles. (We will ignore, for the moment at least, any suggestion that the red grouse might be no more than a sub-species of the willow ptarmigan.) If you want to shoot red grouse you either travel to the wilder parts of Britain and Ireland or you don't shoot them at all, so there is the attraction of exclusivity. Then there is all the history and the tradition associated with grouse shooting. For something like three hundred years writers have been fulsome in their praises of grouse shooting; artists have captured the grouse and its habitat in every medium available and shooting men everywhere – even those who have never set foot on a grouse moor – wake up on the Twelfth of August and look at the weather with an eye to how well the day will suit the opening of the shooting season.

For those who are fortunate enough to take part in grouse shooting, whether as a Gun, a loader, a beater or a picker-up, there is the sheer joy of being out on the moors among the heather and bilberry; of feeling the wind (and quite possibly the rain) in their faces, of hearing the call of the old cock as he leads his covey away from – or directly into – danger and the crack of the guns as that same covey crosses the line. There is the uncertainty every year of not knowing whether the season will be a bumper year or a disaster: an uncertainty that springs from the fact that the grouse is a truly wild quarry and not something that is produced to order in an incubator and on a rearing field. There is the apparently inexorable decline in the grouse population that lends an element of 'last chance' to each shooting season. And for some there is the sheer cost of grouse shooting: a factor that may make it even more desirable in the eyes of those who, proverbially, know the cost of everything and the value of nothing.

The close season for red grouse ends on the Twelfth of August ahead of all other British game birds with the exception of the snipe (if you consider snipe as a game bird). Therefore the start of the grouse season marks the day for many Guns when they are going shooting again for the first time since the close of the pheasant and partridge season on 1 February. There is nothing like an enforced absence to restore one's

A covey of grouse swinging over the butts.

keenness and many a Gun who was feeling jaded at the end of January will be raring to go by the time August comes around. For most Guns grouse shooting is also associated with a holiday and time spent away from the pressures of everyday life. There was a time until quite recently when it was practically impossible to be contacted once away from the lodge and out on the hill, but sadly the curse of the mobile phone has brought an end to that happy state of affairs.

No matter what your individual motivation; no matter whether you are a Gun paying a fortune to take part; a beater receiving a modest remuneration in return for walking miles over rough country; a keeper anxious to provide the best sport possible for his Guns or a moor owner hoping against hope that this year will be the one that marks an upturn in numbers; the grouse occupies a unique position at the pinnacle of shooting sports in the British Isles. It can bring joy and despair in equal measure to Guns, keepers and moor owners alike, though not always for the same reasons. A day that puts a stream of strong coveys over the line will delight the keeper and the moor owner, but may leave the individual Gun who has expended several boxes of cartridges with minimal effect feeling more than a little frustrated at his own performance.

The true joy of grouse shooting is not just the chance to test one's skill with a shotgun against a demanding quarry, the very real physical challenge of tramping for miles over rough ground when walking up or beating, the superb vistas of mountain and moorland that are the natural habitat of the red grouse or the opportunity to take part in a centuries-old ritual that may well be lost to us in the not too distant future. Rather it is a combination of all of these things coupled to something deep within our psyche that is drawn to wild places, and wild creatures and to our basic hunting instinct. If, over the following chapters I can bring to life something of the joy, the satisfaction, the frustration and the despair that grouse shooting can engender then I hope that I will have succeeded in my aims in writing this book.

Footnote.
In the chapters that follow I tend to refer to dogs, dog handlers, Guns and keepers as 'he', 'him', etc, rather than using clumsy, but politically correct terminology such as 'he or she', and 'her or him'. I have used the masculine rather than the feminine because, with the exception of the dogs, shooting tends to be predominantly a male preoccupation. I am aware that some politically correct readers may find this offensive and for those that do let me offer the Rhett Butler apology, viz 'Frankly, I just don't give a d*mn.' For the rest, please understand that 'he' includes 'she' and 'his' includes 'hers' except where it obviously doesn't.

The Grouse

When the subject of grouse shooting in Britain and Ireland is raised it will normally be assumed to involve the red grouse (*Lagopus lagopus scoticus*) rather than one of the other members of the grouse family that are native to these islands. The three others are the black grouse (*Tetrao tetrix*), the ptarmigan (*Lagopus mutus*) and the capercaillie (*Tetrao urogallus*). Three of the four species are legal quarry for the sportsman, outside their various close seasons, but the capercaillie now has such a tenuous hold on existence in Britain that it is no longer on the sportsman's list. Black grouse and ptarmigan are still pursued where they exist in sufficient numbers, though generally, where they are shot, the number killed will be subject to strict self-imposed limits so as not to threaten such viable populations as remain.

It is generally accepted that there are seventeen or eighteen species of grouse and one hundred and twenty-nine sub-species worldwide. Five (or, as we shall see, arguably six) of these species are found in Europe: the four already mentioned plus the hazel grouse (*Bonasa bonasia*) and the willow ptarmigan (*Lagopus lagopus*). While the hazel grouse certainly does not occur in Britain there is some debate about the presence of the willow ptarmigan.

It has long been maintained by most sportsmen and many ornithologists that the red grouse is unique to Britain and Ireland. However, there is an opposing school of thought that holds the view that the red grouse is not a species in its own right but merely a sub-species of the willow ptarmigan. Indeed, there are those who contend that it is not even a sub-species, considering 'red grouse' to be no more than a local name for the willow ptarmigan population of the British Isles. While I am neither a scientist nor an ornithologist it seems to me that there are a couple of clear flaws in this particular argument.

The preferred habitat of the willow ptarmigan, as the name implies, is in the moist areas where willow trees and shrubs thrive. It is found right across northern Europe, North America and northern Asia, living on the Arctic tundra, the Russian steppes and in the Baltic countries. Willow ptarmigan seek shelter during the winter in the cover of the forests of willows, birches, alder, aspen and conifers and sometimes on farmland. Like their cousin the ptarmigan (also known as the rock ptarmigan) their wings are white in summer, while virtually their whole plumage turns white in winter.

Contrast this with the red grouse which lives exclusively on heather moorland and stays the same colour the whole year round. Now, I will concede that technically, the scientists may be right and red grouse may really be no more than willow ptarmigan masquerading under an assumed name, but I prefer to think of them, as I have always thought of them, as game birds that are exclusively and gloriously natives of Scotland, England, Ireland and Wales. And, let us be honest, it really doesn't matter whether the red grouse is a sub-species or a species in its own right. Mention the red grouse to a shooting man anywhere in the world and he will immediately think of heather moorland, of Scotland, England, Ireland and Wales, of a sporting quarry that is among the best and most exclusive (and yes: most expensive) in the world. I can guarantee that he will not respond by saying 'red grouse? Oh, you mean the willow ptarmigan.'

To return to my earlier statement then, if the red grouse is worthy of recognition as a species in its own right there are six species of grouse found in Europe. If you prefer to regard it as a sub-species of the willow ptarmigan then there are only five. When this book is published though I can guarantee that it will not be called *Willow Ptarmigan Shooting*. So, with that out of the way, let us take a look at the life and times of the grouse.

The Red Grouse

Distribution

The red grouse is native to Britain and Ireland. It is found only on land that is primarily

Hen red grouse.

heather moorland and its range has contracted considerably over the past hundred and fifty years or so. There were once viable populations in such places as Exmoor and Dartmoor in the southwest, up through the northern English moors to the lowlands and Highlands of Scotland, the hills of Wales and the bogs of Ireland and some of the Scottish Isles. From much of that former habitat it is now gone, or exists in only tiny fractions of its former numbers, but it still thrives on the hills and moors of northern England and Scotland. In the latter part of the nineteenth century attempts were made to introduce grouse to various locations that were considered by the Victorian sportsmen to provide suitable habitat, including the heathlands of Norfolk and even as far afield as parts of Belgium, Germany and Sweden but as far as I am aware none of these introductions were a long term success.

Today there are still a few grouse to be found on the moors of southwest England and in parts of Wales though they are considered as an endangered species in both areas. In Ireland, where the red grouse was once common, it is also becoming increasingly rare though there are still a few areas that harbour good numbers of birds. It is the great expanses of moorland in the north of England and in Scotland where the red grouse has its strongholds, though in recent years there has been a serious decline in grouse numbers in many parts of Scotland. The grouse is more common on the eastern side of Scotland where the drier climate and superior quality of heather allows for much denser populations to survive, but it can also be found in the Inner and Outer Hebrides, Orkney and parts of Shetland. Estimates of the total red grouse population vary considerably, with some justification, since grouse numbers are subject to cyclical variations. The Game and Wildlife Conservation Trust suggest that the current breeding stock of red grouse in Britain is around a quarter of a million pairs and given the serious scientific basis of the work done by that body it is probably as accurate a figure as it is possible to quote.

Appearance

The red grouse is a medium-sized game bird, slightly bigger than a partridge and considerably smaller than a pheasant. The plumage is a rich reddish-brown with the cocks being generally, though not invariably, darker than the hens as well as being slightly bigger when fully grown. In flight they give the impression of being mostly brown with flashes of white under the wings, but close examination of the plumage reveals a rich variety of colours. The feathers are barred with black and flecked with white particularly underneath the body. The eyes are surrounded by white 'spectacles' and have a bright red comb above them in both males and females, though that of the male is bigger and considerably more prominent particularly during the breeding season. Their legs and feet are covered with white feathers right down to the toes: indeed, the name '*lagopus*' derives from the Greek *lagos* meaning 'hare' and *pus* meaning 'foot'.

Seen up close the red grouse is a striking bird. The sheer variety of shades from a

light grey–brown right through to black, offset with flecks of white and highlighted with the scarlet comb are truly beautiful. To the grouse though, the purpose of this richness and variety of colouring is not beauty but camouflage.

Living on open moorland with no trees or bushes to allow them to roost out of reach of foxes and other four-footed predators, and only the heather to conceal them from eagles, hawks, falcons, buzzards and crows, the grouse is utterly dependent on its ability to crouch unseen in the slightest of cover to protect it from its many enemies. There is no better way to appreciate the sheer perfection of this disguise than to hunt a moor with a pointer or setter in July and August when the young broods of grouse are sitting tightly.

Pointing dogs find their quarry using scent and scent alone. They have no need to catch even the slightest glimpse of a grouse or a covey to know with absolute certainty that the birds are there. The slightest whiff of body scent drifting back on the wind can stop a galloping pointer dead in its tracks. Walk in with the dog handler as the dog rodes forward to flush the birds and in nine cases out of ten the very first indication that you will have of the presence of one bird, or a pair, or even a covey of a dozen or more will be when they burst into the air, possibly from right under your feet. It doesn't matter whether the heather is knee high (when you might reasonably expect not to see them) or barely long enough to cover the soles of your boots. Unless the grouse run across freshly burnt ground where there is no cover at all it is almost certain that you will not spot them at all until the moment they rise into the air. And at times a covey can even run across burnt ground without being seen, impossible though it might seem to the inexperienced eye.

Anyone who has worked as a picker-up on a grouse shoot will know how hard it can be to find shot birds, no matter how good a mark may have been made of the fall. A bird that has enough life left to tuck down into the heather after falling is virtually invisible to the eye, though fortunately, all too obvious to the experienced nose of a gundog. It may seem strange that the reds, russets, browns and blacks of the grouse's plumage can conceal it so well in heather that is predominantly dark green with purple flowers in season, but there is something about the play of light and shade through the foliage that makes it the perfect camouflage.

There can be considerable differences in colouration between individuals and possibly between populations in different parts of the country. The overall impression of the plumage can vary from a deep, rich chestnut to a light, almost grey shade of brown, though no matter how dark or light the colour closer examination will always reveal considerable variety of shade and hue. The bright red comb is especially prominent in the cock bird during the spring but is also present, though generally smaller and less vivid in colour, in the hen grouse. The chicks when first hatched are like fluffy bumble bees, covered in yellow fluff, barred with brown stripes but quickly mature and become fully fledged within just a few weeks. By the beginning of August well grown grouse chicks can be virtually indistinguishable from their parents unless subject to close examination.

Cock and hen grouse paired off in springtime.

Habits

Grouse pair off in the autumn when the cocks seek to establish a territory on which the pair will nest and raise their young in the spring. Territories are fought over and defended quite aggressively, particularly where populations are dense, and cocks that fail to secure a territory are forced to move off to poorer quality ground and may die during the winter. During harsh weather grouse will form packs and sometimes move en masse from their normal haunts when intense cold or heavy snowfall strikes. Severe weather would once have seen them moving down onto farmland, but with the spread of afforestation in the twentieth century they are more likely now to seek shelter among commercial forestry plantations. Once the weather improves the survivors return to the moor or hill. Packing can take place several times in the course of a winter depending on the weather, but by early spring the birds will normally be settled on their territories and preparing to breed.

The nests are rudimentary affairs consisting of little more than a hollow under the heather, though they are remarkably difficult to find. Grouse lay up to a dozen, and sometimes even more, mottled, red–brown eggs, the number probably being dependent on the condition of the hen bird at laying time. The eggs hatch in late May with the chicks being mobile from the moment they emerge from the egg. Although for most of its life the red grouse exists almost entirely on a vegetarian diet of heather leaves and flowers, supplemented with berries in summer, during the first fortnight after hatching the chicks need a diet of protein-rich insect food in order to thrive. Bad weather at this time can decimate broods since, without the necessary insect larva to sustain them, many chicks simply starve to death.

Those that survive mature rapidly – perhaps more rapidly than any other game bird. In a good year chicks that hatch in late May can be virtually indistinguishable from their parents by mid-August when a covey takes to the wing. It is not unusual for a pair to raise as many as ten or a dozen chicks, though the number of chicks that reach maturity will depend on many different factors, including the weather, the quality and quantity of food available, the condition of the parents in springtime, the levels of predation and the amount of disturbance suffered from shepherds and their dogs, hikers, deer and sheep, etc. When young coveys are forced to scatter there is always a danger that not all the chicks will succeed in re-joining the parent birds – and for a grouse chick alone on the moor the odds against survival are extremely high.

The birds stay together in their family groups until the autumn, when large numbers of grouse (if you are fortunate enough to have large numbers of grouse) can come together in the packs previously mentioned. Depending on the weather these packs may stay together for some time, or they may break up again as birds pair off and begin to establish the territories where they will, hopefully, raise their broods in the spring.

Population Dynamics

As has already been noted the red grouse is subject to cyclical variations in its population. It is relatively easy to chart grouse numbers over the past hundred and fifty years or so because reliable and accurate figures exist in the form of game registers and sporting diaries. In many cases estates will have game records running season by season from the mid-nineteenth century right up to the present day, and the numbers of grouse shot each year provide as good as picture as it is possible to get of the annual rise and fall of the population.

There are a few caveats to be borne in mind when drawing up charts of annual grouse bags. It is obviously important that like is compared with like. Does the estate cover the same area of ground throughout the period? Many estates have been broken up with beats being sold off over the years. How much of the ground that remains is still grouse moor? Vast areas have been planted with trees or 'improved' by liming, draining and reseeding to turn heather moorland into pasture. Invasion by bracken may have brought about a considerable reduction in the acreage available to the grouse. The effort put into vermin control and heather burning may have risen or fallen over time.

That said, year on year bag records do provide excellent sources of data to use when building up a picture of the changing pattern of grouse numbers. It is generally true that, ever since the red grouse has been 'managed' rather than simply harvested as a wild crop, the numbers of birds shot in any one season will be directly related to the

Picker-up taking a grouse from her Labrador.

numbers on the ground. In case that sounds like a statement of the blindingly obvious let me explain in a little more detail.

It is well known, and has been for many years, that if too large a population of grouse is left on the ground at the end of the shooting season, it is likely that disease will decimate them during the following spring and early summer. In a good year therefore it is usual to arrange extra shooting days and make every effort to kill as many grouse as possible in order to reduce the risk of a population crash the following year. In the same way, when numbers are low many moors will not be shot at all in order to preserve a nucleus for breeding stock. Thus bag numbers can exaggerate both the highs and the lows of grouse populations, in that a year when no birds were shot does not mean that no birds were on the ground, while a bumper year may have occurred because a higher than usual proportion of the stock was killed. Even so, bag records still provide us with as good a picture of the changes in the grouse population as it is possible to get.

A pointer at work on the moors on a sunny autumn day.

At the beginning of the nineteenth century, before the spread of the railways, simply getting to the moors was a difficult and time-consuming task. Roads were poor, accommodation, where any was available, was often rudimentary, and little effort was made to manage the grouse other than shooting or trapping birds for sport or food. The more accessible areas might be shot quite heavily, while remoter regions were left untouched. At first there was more ground than there were shooting parties to exploit it, but that soon changed. Once improvements in roads, railways and shipping made it possible to reach the moors relatively easily and Victorian fashion started the rush to the Highlands of Scotland, far more attention began to be paid to keepering and managing the hills and moors.

There are two main ways in which conditions can be improved so as to favour the grouse. Burning (muirburn) encourages the growth of nutritious young heather that can sustain a far greater number of birds per acre than moorland where the plant is left to grow unchecked. Controlling those species that prey on grouse and grouse chicks ensures that a larger surplus is left for the sportsman when the season opens. In other words, killing off the grouse's enemies while enhancing its food supply will lead to bigger bags. As grouse shooting grew in popularity and sportsmen began to look for ways to improve the productivity of their moors heather burning and predator control became ever more widespread.

The burning of heather in the late winter and early spring gets rid of old, woody growth and both allows the old root stocks to put out new shoots and encourages the germination of heather seeds. (There is research being carried out now into exposing heather seeds to smoke in order to improve the germination rate when re-seeding.) Where once the heather was burnt pretty much at random in order to provide a fresh bite for grazing animals, the Victorian sportsmen developed a more structured approach specifically to benefit the grouse.

Grouse prefer fresh new heather shoots for food, but also need longer heather to give them shelter from predators and the weather and to provide well-concealed nest sites. When the birds are selecting territories they naturally prefer areas where both types of heather are available in close proximity. If the heather is burnt in vast blocks the grouse will only find the right combination of cover and food around the edges of the burnt areas. By burning in strips and creating a patchwork of long and short heather across the moor many more viable territories are created and more grouse can breed.

At the same time that a more scientific approach to muirburn brought about a huge increase in the number of territories available to the grouse a similar rise in the numbers of gamekeepers employed resulted in a reduction in all the species that preyed on the birds. Keepers in the nineteenth and early twentieth century had very few constraints either on the species they were allowed to kill or the methods by which they could kill them. Shooting, trapping, snaring, poisoning, destruction of nests and the use of terriers to kill foxes and badgers underground were all accepted as simply a normal part of the keepers' work.

Burning the heather produces the fresh young growth that is the preferred diet of the red grouse.

The rich and varied plumage of the red grouse can be seen in these birds lying on top of a butt at the end of a drive.

On many – perhaps the majority – of hills and moors the keepering staff were left to carry out their work without any form of supervision for most of the year. Their success was judged primarily on the numbers of grouse available when the shooting parties arrived in August and September. For a keeper whose home and job were both reliant on having a good show of birds in the shooting season the very idea of predation by beak, talons or teeth was abhorrent. In addition, many keepers relied on 'vermin money' to supplement their wages. Bounties were paid on some estates for every predator that was killed and some of the nineteenth-century records of the numbers of predators destroyed by gamekeepers are almost unbelievable.

Indeed, there must be an element of doubt about some of the very high numbers of eagles, buzzards, hawks and falcons supposedly slaughtered by Victorian game-keepers. Certainly on many estates no predators of any kind were permitted to survive without being harassed at every turn by the keepering staff. I can see where it might have been possible to kill a great many predators when keepering was first started on a moor, but once the initial cull had been made it is harder to understand where the birds and animals to fill the keeper's vermin book would have come from in subsequent years. While I do not doubt that large numbers of eagles, buzzards, harriers, peregrines, ospreys, kestrels and the like were killed by those nineteenth-century keepers, I have a strong suspicion that reports of those numbers were sometimes inflated considerably by the need to convince an absentee employer that the keeper was doing his job properly and to maintain the size of his vermin bonus.

That said, there is no doubt that the twin changes of proper heather burning and what was then considered as 'proper' keepering brought about a rapid and very large explosion in the population of the red grouse. Bag records for many estates in the latter part of the nineteenth century show the number of birds being killed rising enormously from the figures of earlier years. There are other reasons for this beyond the simple fact of an increase in the number on the ground. The change from shooting over dogs to driving the moors was not only a consequence of the increase in grouse numbers to a level that made driving practical but also a reason why grouse bags rose at this time. Shooting over pointers is a relaxed and leisurely way of killing grouse with the bag size being limited by the fitness of both the Guns and the dogs, the weight of the bag that they are prepared to carry and the relatively restricted firepower available. When a small army of beaters are doing the legwork, and perhaps a dozen sportsmen are shooting with double guns with a cart on hand to carry the bag back to the lodge it is much easier to make a big bag.

However, despite the extra inputs of labour, money and scientific research being devoted to the welfare of the grouse it soon became evident that simply burning the heather and killing the predators would not guarantee big bags of grouse year after year. Numbers would rise for a few years and then fall back again – sometimes in spectacular fashion. As we have already seen bad weather in the spring especially in the first few days after the hatch can kill many chicks from exposure or starvation due to a lack of insect food. An infestation of heather beetle can destroy vast acreages of the heather and deprive the birds of their staple diet. Exceptionally severe weather in the winter can force birds to migrate to less harsh areas from which they may not return to their original territories. And, most spectacularly in terms of population crashes, an attack of disease can virtually wipe out the red grouse over a single winter and spring.

An outbreak of 'disease' as far as the red grouse is concerned normally refers to an infestation of the strongyle worm (*Trichostrongylus tenuis*) and this disease is commonly called strongylosis. The strongyle worm is a parasitic threadworm that lives in the gut of the grouse and, in the case of an acute infestation, can severely weaken and eventually kill its host. The strongyle larvae are found on the tips of heather shoots from

where they are eaten by the grouse. They make their way through the gut to the caeca where they grow into adult worms, mate and lay eggs that are excreted by the grouse in their caecal droppings. The eggs hatch into larvae and grow initially within the droppings, then make their way by 'swimming' in a film of water up onto the heather where they are eaten by the grouse to continue the cycle.

A moor that is badly hit by disease is a pitiful sight with dead grouse and sick birds that are too weak to fly littering the heather. As with most parasites, a small number of strongyle worms may have little effect on the health of their host. The simple cycle of ingestion of larvae followed by excretion of eggs followed by further ingestion of larvae means that the greater the density of population of the grouse the greater the worm burden is likely to become. Thus an exceptionally good year when large numbers of birds are left at the end of the season is liable to be followed by an attack of disease and a population crash during the winter, spring and early summer of the next year.

Where it is possible to present grouse populations graphically, using game records, information from grouse counts and so on the graph will usually show a fairly regular cycle of highs and lows in the population with roughly six to eight years between population peaks. This cycle is never perfectly regular since a number of outside influences inevitably skews it. Poor weather at hatching time, a rise in predation, years when shooting is curtailed because of bad weather or some other factor, disease, migration, heather beetle, an increase in grazing pressure and the like can all interfere with the cycle as can such major outside events such as the two World Wars of the twentieth century which saw a dramatic reduction in the efforts expended on keepering and moor management as well as a considerable reduction in shooting. Overall though, when like is compared with like, a pattern will generally emerge of a regular rise and fall in grouse stocks.

On top of this cyclical rise and fall there is also a dramatic reduction in grouse numbers overall. Most charts of grouse populations will show them rising to a peak in the middle to late nineteenth century and then slowly but steadily declining ever since. There will usually be a sharp fall over the war years followed by a return to near pre-war figures, but the overall direction is almost inevitably downwards.

There are many possible causes for this decline and a great deal of research has been carried out over the past hundred years or so to try and identify them and find ways to reverse the trend. Various theories have been put forward to account for the decline – disease, habitat loss, predation, acid rain, global warming, ticks, heather beetles and over-grazing by sheep and deer – and it is likely that all of these things and others have contributed in some degree. One thing that is clear is that, as yet, there is no sure way to reverse the decline, no formula that keepers and estate owners can follow with any certainty that they will bring back the grouse in viable numbers.

When comparing grouse numbers now with the numbers that were found one hundred to one hundred and fifty years ago it is important to realise that like is not being compared with like. The beginning of proper heather burning coupled to rigorous predator control had given the grouse an unprecedented boost by greatly improving its habitat at the same time as keepers were removing most of the non-human species that preyed on them. Populations reached levels that were probably never really sustainable in the long term. As to why the decline in numbers seems to be ongoing despite all the efforts of keepers, estate owners and scientists, there is probably no simple answer but rather a combination of factors that will vary in their relative importance from moor to moor. Let us consider some of the probable reasons for the fall in grouse numbers and how they may interact with each other.

There is no questioning the fact that vast areas of heather moorland have been lost over the past hundred years or so. Tens of thousands of acres have been planted with trees and thousands more acres have been limed and re-seeded to turn them into pasture for grazing animals. In many cases the trees would have little or no economic value were it not for the grants and tax breaks that were provided by successive governments to encourage the forestry industry. Indeed, in some areas in the far north of Scotland where neither the soil nor the climate was in any way conducive to forestry in the first place, the stunted trees that have grown are worth nothing since the cost of extracting them would far exceed the value of the timber produced.

'Improving' moorland to make grass parks for sheep has not been an unqualified success either since much of the 'improved' land became sour and boggy growing mainly rushes and poor quality grasses. That said, the moorland that was converted to grass tended to be marginal ground anyway, generally on the edges of the moor, and in some cases may have been a positive benefit to the grouse because it reduced the grazing pressure on the heather at certain times of the year. It is less easy to find something positive to say about forestry, at least from the point of view of the red grouse.

In many cases vast forestry blocks took over whole grouse moors. Once the land has been ploughed and planted and the trees have reached five or six feet in height the moor is effectively lost to the grouse forever. This overall planting tended to be more common where estates were purchased specifically for afforestation, with sporting estates being more likely to allocate parts of the ground to trees with the better areas of moorland being retained for sporting purposes. In theory this may have seemed like a sensible move, the trees (or the grants and tax breaks associated with them) boosting the cash flow for the estate while reserving the best parts of the land for shooting and stalking. In practice the outcome was often less positive than had been anticipated.

One obvious problem with creating large areas of dense tree cover is that the trees provide strongholds for crows and foxes. Open heather moorland provided few nesting sites for crows and keepers generally knew every tree where a nest could be built making it a relatively simple matter in the spring to shoot the adults or destroy the nests. Confronted with ten thousand acres of almost impenetrable spruce and larch there is simply no way of eradicating crows. They incubate their eggs and rear their young safe from even the most determined assault.

In the same way, an experienced keeper would once have known the location of every fox den on his beat and visited each one with his terriers at cubbing time. With the advent of forestry though foxes were presented with thousands and thousands of acres of sheltered housing projects. To make matters worse, all too often these reservoirs of vermin would be situated right on the edge of the grouse moor giving the predators a safe haven only a matter of yards from the scene of their depredations. Certainly, keepers have adapted to try and cope with these problems. Larsen traps for crows and lamping foxes helps to keep some sort of control as we will see in a later chapter, but forestry has certainly tilted the odds very much in the direction of the predators.

Breaking up what were once huge tracts of moorland with blocks of trees may also have had a bad effect on the grouse. Though largely sedentary and territorial, grouse are believed by many observers to 'migrate' when bad weather or population pressure cause problems locally. I suspect that this may have been an easier option for them when moorlands ran unbroken for many miles, unlike today when the land is split between heather and timber. Instead of being able to move a little bit at a time, with birds drifting almost imperceptibly from one area to another, crossing ten thousand acres of forestry means making a conscious decision to leave one stretch of moorland and go to seek another.

Although a lot of the areas given over to forestry will have been on the less productive (in terms of grouse numbers) parts of the moors planting over these marginal areas may have done more damage to the grouse population than might have been expected. In very dry summers grouse may move from the parts of the hill where the best heather grows down into wet, boggy and rushy parts in search of water and insect life for their chicks. If all the poorer ground has been covered with trees this option is denied them. Restricting the area available to the grouse to spread into during good years also increases the population density on the ground making it easier for disease to take hold.

It is likely therefore that the spread of forestry has done more damage to the red grouse than simply removing large areas of their habitat. Tree planting has made it easier for predators like crows and foxes to thrive around the edges of moorland and in many cases taken away the option of birds moving onto wetter ground during times of drought. Pockets of moorland surrounded by trees may be less able to support their isolated populations of grouse than in the days when moors ran uninterrupted for mile after mile. However, it is clear that forestry alone is not responsible for the decline in grouse numbers.

Two other candidates often mentioned are the tick and the heather beetle. The past ten to fifteen years has seen the latter insect wreak havoc on many moors in Scotland, particularly in the far north. The heather beetle (*Lochmaea suturalis*) larvae eats the heather leaving characteristic reddish-brown patches as the heather dies off. Burning the dead heather will assist in its regeneration, but there is a danger, especially in wetter areas, that the new heather may be choked out by white grass, particularly if the beetle larvae continue their depredations on the fresh shoots.

It is possible that the amount of damage caused by the heather beetle has been

Forestry plantation encroaching around the edges of the moor.

worse in recent years because of a series of mild winters. It is said by many keepers that a severe winter with prolonged spells of hard frost kills off the beetles and their larvae. I am not sure if this has been proven scientifically, but certainly the damage caused by the heather beetle appears to have reached unprecedented proportions during the last few years when winters have been relatively mild.

Ticks also seem to have become more common during the past few years and again it seems possible that this may be as a result of mild winter conditions. Ticks affect grouse numbers in two ways: they spread louping ill, a disease which can be fatal for grouse and, where tick burdens are particularly heavy, they can actually kill grouse chicks by the sheer weight of infestation. Incidentally, tick bites can also cause humans to fall victim to Lyme disease; a particularly nasty, debilitating condition that can cause meningitis, arthritis, heart problems and neurological disorders.

Ticks are blood-sucking parasites carried by sheep, deer and hares as well as grouse, and some success has been reported with using sheep as 'tick mops' to reduce the number of ticks on the moors. The sheep must be treated regularly with acaricides – dips or pour-on treatments that kill any ticks that attempt to use the sheep as hosts – and moved around the moor in order to mop up as many ticks as possible. Research from the Game and Wildlife Conservation Trust suggests that this approach may be effective provided that the deer and hare population is not too high so that the ticks have too many untreated hosts on which to prey. It is not a cheap option, since the sheep need regular dosing if they are not to simply act as another host for the ticks and exacerbate the problem rather than cure it.

Other candidates that I have heard suggested as culprits for the decline in grouse numbers are acid rain, and, almost inevitably such is its 'popularity' as a cause of all evils at the moment, global warming. My own feeling is that there is no single factor that has caused the decline in grouse numbers. Loss of habitat and isolation of moorland areas has certainly contributed, increases in predation and attacks by heather beetle and ticks will be factors that vary in significance from moor to moor, and it is possible that there is some wider factor at work as well. It is also possible that the extremely high numbers of grouse found in the late nineteenth and early twentieth centuries were never sustainable in the long term.

While there is no doubt that the red grouse has suffered a serious decline in parts of the British Isles, particularly in Wales, Ireland and, more recently, in some areas of Scotland, the picture is not one of universal doom and gloom. Many moors in northern England and some parts of Scotland still have thriving populations of grouse. In a good year – and there are still good years – the most pressing problem for some moor owners may be that it becomes difficult to kill enough grouse to stave off the risk of disease caused by over-crowding. A great deal of research and experimentation is going on to try and discover the cause and the cure for declining numbers in less fortunate areas. While never likely to occur again in the numbers that were around a century ago the red grouse is still widespread and locally abundant.

The Black Grouse

The black grouse is a slightly larger bird than the red grouse and is more likely to be found around the margins of moorland where there are farms and woodland rather than right out on the open hill. Overall they are much less common than they were a hundred years ago having disappeared from many areas as heathlands were ploughed up for arable farming, but in places where the right conditions exist for them they can still be found in good numbers. Taken over the whole of the UK though the species is considered to be in danger and there are a number of action plans and conservation projects aimed at arresting their decline.

The male is called a blackcock and the female a greyhen (collectively they are often referred to as blackgame) and, unlike the red grouse the sexes are readily distinguished by their plumage. The male is primarily black, with bright red wattles over the eyes, a white rump and white stripes along the wings that show particularly when the bird is

Black grouse. (PHOTO: LAURIE CAMPBELL)

in flight. Adult males have a distinctive lyre-shaped tail that they fan out as part of their courtship display when trying to attract females to mate. The female is much more like the red grouse in appearance, though slightly larger and with a stronger beak. Their plumage is a grey-brown overall, though as with the red grouse, close examination shows considerable variety in colouration and pattern.

The initial courtship of black grouse is a communal affair with the males gathering at sites called 'leks' and posturing, mock-fighting and strutting around displaying their plumage. All this is watched, often with little sign of interest, by the greyhens. Once they have mated the hens find nest sites, usually among long heather to provide them with cover, lay their eggs and incubate them until they hatch in June. The chicks are mobile as soon as they leave the egg and will follow the hen as she leads them in search of insects, caterpillars and the like to provide them with the protein-rich diet that they need during their first couple of weeks.

As they mature they will live on catkins, shoots, buds, seeds, grasses and berries according to season, and they particularly like the margins of moors and forests where there is access to farmland. In the days when corn was cut by scythe or binder and left to ripen in stooks black grouse flighting down to feed on the sheaves was a familiar, and probably quite annoying, sight in areas where they were plentiful. Lines of blackgame perched along the tops of the stone walls surrounding fields were once a common sight and the subject of a number of paintings. In times of heavy snow they are often seen feeding high up in the branches of trees, eating rowan or hawthorn berries or the buds and catkins of birch, alder and willow.

While it would be difficult to mistake a blackcock in full plumage for a red grouse, it can be quite difficult to make the same distinction when a greyhen rises ahead of a pointing dog. The slightly larger size and somewhat slower wing beat ought to warn the sportsman to hold his fire (unless of course he is on a moor where it is permitted to shoot blackgame, and the opening day of the season, 20 August, has arrived) but it is all too easy in the heat of the moment to raise the gun and pull the trigger before realising that the target is a greyhen and not a red grouse. It is the nature of these things that any such shot fired in error will invariably be fatal.

Gun and loader watch closely as a covey flies over the neighbouring butt.

At first sight the afforestation of moorlands might seem to be advantageous to the black grouse. This may be the case in the first few years with birch, alder, rowan and willow regenerating naturally among the cultivated softwoods, but once the evergreens have gained a bit of height and spread their canopy over the forest floor the native trees are starved of light and die off. Modern forestry design is more sympathetic to the needs of wildlife than was the case in the past, and where native trees are planted or natural regeneration is encouraged around the margins of the commercial planting a habitat suitable for black grouse can be created.

Various studies have taken, and are currently taking, place to try and identify the reasons why blackgame have become an endangered species in some areas where once they were common. Loss of habitat certainly plays a major role as does predation and deaths caused by birds flying into deer fences. The usual suspects, foxes, crows and raptors, all prey on black grouse and on their eggs and chicks, and where numbers have fallen to critical levels predation may be enough to preclude any hope of recovery unless steps are taken to minimise its impact.

Blackgame can still be found, albeit in very low numbers, in parts of Wales. Northern England and Scotland host quite large populations locally but they are no longer found in many of their former haunts such as the brecklands of Norfolk, Cannock Chase, the Peak District and the moors of the south west. That said, there are plans to try and reintroduce this spectacular member of the grouse family to some of its old haunts and it remains to be seen how well these will work out.

The Ptarmigan

Ptarmigan can be found right around the world in the northern hemisphere living on the Arctic coasts, the north American tundra, the Russian steppes, in Greenland and in the Alps and the Pyrenees as well as the higher reaches of the mountains of the Scottish Highlands. In Scotland ptarmigan are normally found on the high tops above the two thousand feet contour, though they are sometimes seen lower down, particularly when they may have been chased off their normal haunts by the attentions of an eagle.

They are very slightly smaller than the red grouse and are quite unmistakeable, particularly in flight. In their summer plumage they are somewhat lighter in colour than the red grouse with a mixture of grey, fawn and white feathers helping them to blend in with the rocks and scree of their chosen habitat. Their wings are white though, and any question of confusing a ptarmigan with a red grouse is dispelled as soon as they take flight. In winter they turn completely white apart from the red wattle above their eyes and a touch of black in their tails.

Whilst the white plumage is obviously an effective camouflage in snow it might seem to be a dangerous colour for the birds when they are on rocks or among the heather, bilberry and crowberry plants that provide them with their main source of food. It is only when you have climbed high up into the mountains and tried to spot ptarmigan that you can appreciate just how effective their plumage is at concealing them, no matter what the time of year. Often the first intimation that there are ptarmigan around will be the sound of their distinctive guttural call – a sort of scraping chuckle.

It can be quite frustrating to hear the call and know that there are ptarmigan running ahead of you through what appears to be either bare rock or heather no more than an inch or so in height and yet still not be able to spot them – until they take flight.

As with the other three British grouse species the ptarmigan is less common than it was in former years. The high tops of the mountains have become much more accessible over the past thirty years or so with ski lifts operating

Ptarmigan. (PHOTO: LAURIE CAMPBELL)

all year round to take walkers high into the hills even in summer, and the popularity of four-wheel drive vehicles meaning that walkers can get much further into mountain areas before they have to abandon their transport and take to their feet. Disturbance is certainly a factor in the ptarmigans' decline with walkers in summer and skiers in winter invading the places where once they lived virtually undisturbed all year round. Collisions with ski lift cables and pylons also account for many deaths each year. Crows and gulls are attracted to these areas by food scraps dumped by the tourists and will, naturally, not be averse to supplementing their diets with the eggs and chicks of nesting ptarmigan.

In the quieter areas of the Highlands they still survive, sometimes in good numbers, though like the red grouse they are subject to seasonal variations in their population. Ptarmigan tend to be either there or not there as far as most sporting estates are concerned in that they are left pretty much to their own devices rather than being managed in the manner of the red grouse population. Certainly the ptarmigan will benefit where predators are properly controlled, but they are generally an incidental species as far as sport is concerned. A stroll with dog and gun around the high tops on a fine summer day in search of ptarmigan may provide excellent sport, and will almost certainly provide a good deal of healthy exercise, but for me, and I suspect for many others, the pleasure of the day will come as much or more from the walk and the scenery as from the chance to shoot a ptarmigan. Indeed, on those odd occasions when I have been ptarmigan shooting I have found that one or two birds in the bag is as many as I want to shoot in a day – after that I would rather just watch them.

One of the most memorable sights I have ever seen on a shooting day was a covey of ptarmigan gliding across the hill with the autumn sunlight reflecting off their wings. There may be prettier sights to be seen in the mountains, but if there are I have yet to experience them.

Capercaillie

The capercaillie is by far the largest member of the grouse family with a mature cock weighing as much as eight to ten pounds, though the females are considerably lighter. Once native to Scotland and quite common, they became extinct in that country in 1785. It is alleged that the last pair were shot for a royal wedding banquet at Balmoral, although, since it was 1848 when Queen Victoria and Prince Albert first took out a lease on the estate, the story appears to lack a certain amount of credibility. The Victorians were supposed to like their game to be well hung, but in the absence of refrigeration it seems unlikely that a brace of capercaillie would still be edible after sixty-three years in the game larder.

It is well documented though that several attempts were made to reintroduce the capercaillie to Scotland. The Earl of Fife tried at Mar Lodge but was unsuccessful, then, in 1837, Lord Breadalbane managed to reintroduce them on his estate at Taymouth Castle. The birds were brought across from Sweden by Llewellyn Lloyd and

Capercaillie. (PHOTO: LAURIE CAMPBELL)

a gamekeeper called Larry Banville. Banville kept a detailed journal of their adventures in pursuit of the birds and many years later this was published as *The Banville Diaries* (Collins, 1986). As well as telling the story of the return to Scotland of the capercaillie the book is a fascinating insight into the life and work of a keeper in the nineteenth century.

The reintroduction was successful and started a revival for the capercaillie in Scotland with the population spreading as further areas were colonised both naturally and by further releases of birds, some from overseas and some from descendants of the original birds.

The capercaillie is primarily found in mature, open pine forests or oak woods. The male is almost as big as a turkey with a dark brown back, white flecks on his wings, a dark, metallic green breast and a blue–grey head highlighted by a crimson wattle over the eyes. In contrast the female is not only smaller but much less brightly coloured, being flecked in shades of dark and reddish brown designed to camouflage her when she is sitting on eggs. Like the black grouse the capercaillie has a mating ritual involving the males displaying at traditional lek sites.

The sight and sound of a capercaillie lek is both unmistakeable and unforgettable. The males strut like the turkeys they resemble with their tails erect and fanned out and their wings spread and trailing just above the ground, sometimes performing a 'flutter-jump' that involves leaping into the air flapping their wings and then fluttering back to the ground. These actions are accompanied by the distinctive 'song' of the capercaillie that is like nothing else to be heard in the woods. A series of rattles, gurgles, pops and clops, often described as the sound of a cork being drawn from a bottle, echo through the woods as the males attempt to attract females to watch their display.

While the blackcock lek mainly consists of posturing and display, male capercaillie will actually fight for the opportunity to mate with the females. These contests often result in injury for the birds and at times, even the death of one of the contestants. So aggressive are the males during the mating season that it is not unknown for them to attack humans who intrude on their territories.

The hen lays her eggs in a scrape in the ground and attends to the incubating and the rearing of the chicks with no help from the male bird. As with the other grouse species the chicks are heavily dependent on a protein-rich diet of insects, grubs and caterpillars for the first two or three weeks after hatching after which they are mainly vegetarian in their eating habits. Berries, shoots, buds and flowers are all eaten according to the season, though in winter the birds are largely reliant on the needles of evergreen trees and can do a certain amount of damage by nipping out the growing tips of young pine trees.

Despite their success following their reintroduction in the nineteenth century the capercaillie is once more facing the threat of extinction in Scotland. A number of factors are considered to be responsible for this including all the usual suspects: loss of habitat, predation especially of eggs and young chicks and increased disturbance by humans. A significant number of deaths are caused when birds fly into deer fences. When a capercaillie in full flight strikes a tightly strung deer fence there can only be one winner and it will not be the capercaillie. Ironically, in many cases deer fences are erected with the express intention of excluding deer so that woodlands can regenerate naturally for the benefit of birds like the capercaillie.

In the same vein, efforts made to protect and preserve other rare or endangered species may have also contributed to the downfall of the capercaillie. Pine martens and wildcats, goshawks and sparrowhawks will all prey on capercaillie chicks and young and the eggs are vulnerable to the increasing numbers of hooded and carrion crows that infest the countryside. This conflict in trying to find a balance between endangered species where success for one directly affects the prospects for another is not limited to capercaillie. Pine martens prey on red squirrels for example, and I recently watched a documentary on black grouse where the presenter was excited (and delighted!) to see just how many hen harriers were quartering the moorland on which a few pairs of blackgame were struggling to survive and clearly failed to make any possible connection between the abundance of predators and the absence of prey.

A great deal of effort is currently being made by many individuals and organisations to try to ensure that the capercaillie does not become extinct in Scotland for a second time. In the 1980s the population was estimated to be as high as fifty thousand individuals but by the end of the century this number had dropped to as few as one thousand birds. Most landowners adopted a voluntary moratorium on shooting capercaillie and in 2001 an Amendment (Scotland) to the Wildlife and Countryside Act 1981 formally removed them from the quarry list. Marking or removing deer fences, trapping or shooting such of the capercaillies' predators as may legally be controlled, preserving and improving their remaining habitat and perhaps even repeating the reintroductions that were made almost two hundred years ago will, hopefully, see this magnificent bird returned to a viable basis in Scotland and eventually even parts of England and Wales as well.

Grouse Prospects

Most of the sporting journals and many regular newspapers will carry some form of article around August looking at the prospects for grouse. I have written quite a few of

Present day sportsman armed with an old, percussion muzzle-loading shotgun for a day shooting over pointers.

them myself over the years – sometimes optimistic, sometimes gloomy according to what we have seen during grouse counts and field trials and what other keepers, dog handlers, estate owners and shoot managers have told me. Inevitably there are good years and bad years: sometimes there are excellent stocks of grouse in one part of the country while other areas are cancelling all shooting; sometimes there is cautious optimism and sometimes gloom and doom overall.

It is the nature of the press that in many cases – particularly when the articles are published in newspapers or magazines that have little or no real interest in or knowledge of fieldsports – what is printed is unmitigated rubbish. In this category I include not only the traditional nonsense about 'the crack of high-powered rifles in the glens' but also the well-meant stories that somehow manage to give completely the wrong impression even though author and photographer have actually been out on the moors and seen grouse shooting in action for themselves. It is often said that there is no such thing as bad publicity, but it is difficult to see how some of the nonsense that is printed every August can be in any way beneficial to either the sportsman or the grouse.

Overall it appears that the prospects for grouse in Britain – and 'grouse' in this context includes all four species currently resident here – are best described as mixed. The capercaillie is currently in crisis and may even become extinct within these islands unless research and remedial work can save it. Ptarmigan are doing well enough over much of their range but have suffered locally from the disturbance and associated problems arising from increased access to the high tops. Likewise, black grouse can be found in encouraging numbers in many places but are facing virtual extinction in some areas where they were once abundant.

The red grouse, which is far and away the most important of the four as regards shooting, is also facing the future with differing prospects according to where in the country it resides. Well-keepered moors in the north of England and parts of Scotland are still able to show good numbers of birds in most years. Parts of the Highlands have suffered badly from the ravages of the heather beetle in recent years and there are real fears for the future of the red grouse particularly in the far north. Other factors such as ticks, disease, predation, climate change, increased disturbance by humans, changes in grazing pressure by sheep and deer, habitat loss and fragmentation, the decline in the numbers of keepers employed on moors and legal restrictions on the control of predators have all contributed in some degree to the general decline of the grouse.

This bridge trap is intended to kill small ground predators such as stoats and weasels.

Economically the red grouse is probably too important to the countryside to be allowed to decline without considerable efforts being made on its behalf by those of us with sporting interests. Capercaillie and blackgame, though of less importance as sporting birds, are sufficiently iconic to attract the attentions of other conservation-minded bodies such as the RSPB who are working hard to preserve their status. The ptarmigan, if left undisturbed in the high and lonely places where it makes its home, will probably survive okay, though if the doom-laden prophecies of the climate change lobby are correct the high tops may eventually be covered with tropical forests.

Taken over the past couple of centuries there is no question that grouse numbers in Britain and Ireland have declined steadily and in the case of the capercaillie, catastrophically. Whether further decline is inevitable it is difficult to say. Certainly a great deal of money is being devoted to research and to practical measures to try and arrest that decline and more enlightened attitudes to the preservation of moorland may help in that respect. Man brought about an explosion in the grouse population at the beginning of the nineteenth century when moorland began to be managed for sporting purposes. Man is probably also responsible for the steady decline in grouse numbers since around the beginning of the twentieth century. It remains to be seen to what extent, if at all, Man will be able to arrest that decline in the years to come.

History

G rouse must have been hunted by man for food for about as long as both species have existed together on this planet. This is hardly surprising since a grouse of whatever species comprises a decent-sized chunk of edible protein, and is often found living in areas where food of any kind is difficult to come by. Hunting grouse for sport is a more recent development though and dates from the period when man began to be sufficiently well organised to have spare time available that needed to be filled by some form of what is now sometimes referred to as 'leisure activity'. A hungry man hunts with little beyond the end result in mind. He wants to put food on the table, or perhaps on the floor of the cave. A man who is hunting for sport is generally more concerned with methods than with results.

Take the trout fisherman as an example. If you have an area of water from which you wish to extract a trout or two the simplest way (short of tossing in a hand grenade) is probably to drag some sort of net through the water. If you want to catch them with rod and line a worm is generally a fairly effective way of fooling them into swallowing your hook. But no: the trout fisherman restricts himself to trying to persuade the fish to swallow a little bunch of feathers. If he is a real purist he will only use a floating bunch of feathers and only throw it in a particular direction – a dry fly cast upstream - just to make the whole job as difficult as possible. Why? Because there is far greater satisfaction in executing a difficult task with style and panache than in doing something simple and mundane, even though the end result may be the same. In many ways the same 'philosophy' applies to shooting.

The easiest way to kill a pheasant with a shotgun is to blast it while it is on the ground or roosting in a tree – but we don't do that. We go to some trouble to get it up into the air and even then – if we are proper sporting gentlemen – we ignore the relatively easy low flappers and shoot only at the high, difficult birds. The principle behind sporting shooting is to show birds that are difficult enough to test the skills of the Guns, but not so difficult as to be impossible to kill. It is an often-quoted remark that one good high bird is worth a dozen low flappers, but repetition does not take away the essential truth of the statement. Most Shots prefer birds that test them to the limit and there is no doubt that one really spectacular kill on a high curling pheasant will be remembered years later when a hundred more mundane shots have long been forgotten.

The grouse fulfils the requirements of being difficult to kill in more ways than just its speed and curving flight. Unless you happen to live on the fringe of a grouse moor – and most of us do not, grouse moors generally being situated in the wildest, most remote and thus least populated parts of the country – you are likely to have to mount some sort of expedition just to get to where the grouse are in the first place. Today this might mean no more than a few hours in the air-conditioned comfort of a car or an even shorter flip in an aeroplane, but in the early days of grouse shooting reaching the moors from London was a real expedition in every sense of the word.

Larry Banville, the keeper involved in the reintroduction of the capercaillie, records in his diary how in 1822 he was sent to 'make his own way' from London to Bowes Moors in Yorkshire for the opening of the grouse shooting season. Banville walked the whole way – some two hundred and thirty miles – and was there to meet his master, Llewelleyn Lloyd, just seven days later. I assume that Lloyd made the journey by some less strenuous means, perhaps by coach or on horseback since this was a few years before the coming of the railways, though it is also possible that he may have gone by passenger ship. Whatever the means of transport it will have taken him several days though probably not quite as long as Larry Banville tramping the road to the north. Incidentally, though the diary does not record it, if Banville had been accompanied by his team of pointers or setters the walk would have been useful in getting them fit and hardening their feet ready for the hill.

Lloyd and Banville travelled north in order to shoot grouse but long before grouse shooting became possible the red grouse was a natural quarry for the falconer. In one sense this is the literal truth since in the wild grouse are part of the diet of any raptors living on and around grouse moors, but it is also true in a wider sense. The vast open spaces of heather moorland not only allow a falcon to have a clear flight at its quarry but also ensure that the falconer has the best possible view of his bird in action. An adult grouse and a peregrine falcon are a well-matched pair and the result of every flight may be in doubt right up to the end.

A peregrine stooping at – it is often claimed – up to two hundred miles an hour would seem to have every advantage over a grouse flying at perhaps a quarter of that speed. In assessing the odds on the grouse surviving though there is also the matter of manoeuvrability to consider. Just when the peregrine is a few scant feet from the fleeing grouse and a kill seems certain the grouse will twist and jink or perhaps dive down into some long heather and foil the pursuing falcon. Of course there are other times when an audible thump and a flurry of feathers will signal a successful flight, death for the grouse and triumph for the predator over the prey.

Some of the larger falcons and the modern hybrids used for the sport are capable of overhauling a grouse in a straight flight, but the peregrine relies on the combined effect of wing power and gravity to accelerate it up to the speed required to swoop down and kill its prey. A goshawk or Harris hawk can be flown off the wrist at prey such as pheasant, rabbit or hare, and provide challenging sport and a fascinating spectacle in so doing, but working a peregrine on grouse is an altogether more complicated, more interesting and more exciting business.

First you have to find your grouse.

The natural instinct of grouse when they are aware that a peregrine falcon is in the vicinity is to clap down tightly in the heather and rely on their camouflage to conceal them from the predator. As we have already seen in an earlier chapter, the plumage of the red grouse is superbly adapted for just this purpose. A peregrine falcon hunting naturally will fly high above the moor searching for grouse. The bird has much better eyesight than any human, and is looking down from a far better vantage point than a human eye just six feet above the ground. However, the falconer requires more control over his sport than simply to turn a peregrine loose and hope that, somewhere in his vicinity, it might find a grouse to pursue. He wants to control and order the situation. The first problem for the falconer is therefore to find a grouse for his falcon to chase. And this is where dogs enter the equation.

Not just any dogs, but dogs that point game rather than simply flushing it. In Britain until quite recently this meant either pointers or setters, but over the past sixty years or so a number of pointing breeds have been introduced from the continent including German pointers in several varieties, Weimaraners, Hungarian vizslas, Brittany spaniels, Italian Spinones and others. The particular ability of all pointing dogs is that they can locate game by scent alone and, having found birds, will stand motionless – 'on point' – until ordered to go forward and flush the game from its hiding place. Given the combination of grouse that are sitting tightly and a good steady dog it is quite common for several minutes to elapse between the dog first pointing the birds and the birds breaking cover.

When shooting grouse over dogs, as we will see in a later chapter, this gap between finding game and flushing it is essential to allow the Guns to approach to within range of where the birds are hiding. For the falconer it allows time for his peregrine to be released and climb away up into the air above the moor giving it the height necessary for it to be able to stoop on the grouse once they fly.

Pointers and setters were selectively bred over many years to have the qualities needed by falconers, and indeed by anyone seeking to kill grouse by other means, of which more later. They needed, first of all, to have the ability and the inclination to point game – a natural instinct that was honed and enhanced by careful selection and breeding. Then they had to be able to run long distances over rough ground in order to find grouse that were likely to be fairly thinly spread over many, many acres of heather. Finally they needed exceptionally good noses even by canine standards so that they could find birds before they were so close to them that the birds would flush rather than staying put, trusting in their camouflage, and hoping the dog would go away.

It is the natural instinct of red grouse to sit tightly in the presence of a predator, especially in summer and early autumn when they have young broods to protect. An adult grouse and a peregrine are reasonably evenly matched, but young birds are easy prey for the falcon. Other moorland predators such as the hen harrier may not be able

Birds of prey like this peregrine falcon were used to hunt grouse long before the invention of the shotgun.

Pointers are still used to find grouse for falconry as well as for shooting.

to kill grouse in flight, but grouse chicks are especially vulnerable to a harrier as it methodically quarters the moor a few feet above the ground. Once located chicks that are as yet unable to fly are helpless victims for the harrier. With a nest close by in a stand of long heather, the harrier will shuttle back and forth between the covey and its hungry brood, often taking every single grouse chick from the covey. Good camouflage is thus essential to the survival of the grouse, though ironically it is the grouse's reliance on just this defence mechanism that makes it vulnerable to a man with a gun, a net or a falcon.

If grouse behaved like many other birds and flew away when they were first aware of danger, long before any potential predator could come close to them, it would be extremely difficult to hunt them since they tend to be found in such wide-open areas. It is almost impossible for a man to cross heather moorland unseen unless, like the deer stalker, he proceeds for much of the distance flat on his belly. While this does not preclude the stalker from killing his stag, since a red deer is a very large and visible animal that can be shot with a rifle, from a prone position at a distance of several hundred yards, it would make it extremely difficult to for a man to kill a grouse. Late season grouse shooting over dogs may well involve an element of stalking if the gun is to get close enough for a shot, but in general grouse are only vulnerable to falconers and to men shooting over dogs or by walking up because they will sit, more or less

tightly, in the summer and autumn months. Driven shooting is of course another matter, but more of that in our next chapter.

Young grouse, in late July and the early part of August, can sit so tightly and have such reliance on the efficacy of their camouflage that it is not uncommon for them to be pegged on the ground by dogs without even attempting to take to their wings. Indeed, on more than one occasion I have seen a Gun tread on a grouse as he was walking in to a point – and these were fully feathered birds well capable of flight, not young chicks only able to run or hide. The occasional dog can become quite adept at rushing in and grabbing grouse as they take off, though this is not something that will endear them to any but the most bone-headed of handlers. That said, in the days before the invention of the shotgun, a dog that could catch grouse would have been a valuable aid to putting meat on the table.

Killing grouse with a falcon is and was one of the most highly rated forms of field sports. In the Middle Ages such sport was strictly reserved for noblemen: indeed there was a hierarchy that dictated what rank a man must hold in order to own and fly various types of bird of prey. Falconry was then as it is now a sport rather than a means of providing meat but there were other less sporting but more efficient ways of killing grouse for the table. A falcon can kill only one bird out of a covey, and can only fly a limited number of times in any one day. It also requires a skilled trainer and handler and the investment of a considerable amount of time and effort before it can be flown free at wild quarry. A net on the other hand can be made with nothing more than some string and a net needle and a snare is nothing more than a length of wire.

Netting grouse can be done in at least two ways. Grouse tend to fly close to the ground hugging the contours of the hill and are not always particularly good at spotting obstacles in their path. One of the reasons believed to have contributed greatly to the decline of the capercaillie is the tendency of the birds to kill themselves by flying into deer fences. I have on several occasions seen a red grouse killed by flying straight into a wire fence after having been flushed by a pointer – possibly because its attention was more on the dog than on where it was going.

This accidental method of killing grouse was once used deliberately. Grouse tend to fly in fairly predictable lines when flushed – a characteristic that makes the modern sport of driven grouse shooting possible. A fine net strung across a flightline could be deadly and would potentially account for considerable numbers of birds. Richard Kearton, a writer and photographer, published a book called *With Nature and a Camera* in 1897 in which he describes this method of killing grouse. A net about a hundred yards long rising perhaps eight to ten feet in the air is strung across the moor. Kearton shows a photograph of the net in action with the owner extracting a grouse from its meshes. It looks similar to the stake nets that fishermen set on the Solway and other estuaries to catch salmon, sea trout and flatfish. Quite a fine net is held up by a series of widely spaced long poles. Down below a series of short sticks at intervals of a few yards supports the bottom of the net. The book doesn't say what these shorter sticks are for, and the photograph isn't clear enough to see, but I would assume they form some sort of pocket that the birds would drop into after hitting the standing part of the net.

A grouse hitting the net at speed might well be killed or so badly injured as to be unable to run or fly off again, but having a pocket at the foot of the net would make sense because it would effectively trap any birds that hit the net and fell uninjured and would otherwise be able to get up and fly once they had recovered from the initial impact. I have no doubt that a net like this would be an effective means of killing grouse and Kearton records that the owner of the one he photographed had sometimes taken as many as thirty grouse out of one net in a single day. Similar devices known as mist nets are still used under licence by ornithologists catching up birds for scientific research.

The same man who used the nets was also adept at snaring grouse. He would set up to two thousand fine snares made from copper wire along the sheep tracks and other places where grouse would run. These too could be a deadly means of securing a bag of grouse and would have the advantage for a poacher of being less obvious than a length of netting strung across the moor, though a snared grouse, presumably flapping and struggling when first trapped, would be visible at a considerable distance. In fact the man Kearton was describing was not, strictly speaking, a poacher since he apparently owned a small acreage of moorland surrounded by much larger moors and though not popular with his neighbours his methods were still legal at that time.

The more commonly described method of netting grouse, and one that is mentioned in virtually every book about pointers and setters, was to net the grouse after using a pointing dog to find them. The principle seems to have been to run a dog until it pointed a covey of birds, then have two men draw a length of net right over the dog and the birds. This may seem far-fetched to anyone who has not seen for themselves just how tightly grouse will sit, but I have no doubt that it was another effective means of killing grouse, though it would only have been viable for just a few weeks in late July and early August when the young birds were still sitting tightly but had grown enough to be worth taking.

Setters were supposed to have been better for this than pointers because of the way they 'sett' game. A pointer tends to stand up tall when he is on point, but setters are more prone to crouch down and this would make it easier to draw the net right over the dog. In order to work in this way the grouse would have to be very close to the dog when pointed and when scent is strong this is not always the case. I have never seen anyone trying to net grouse – indeed, it would be illegal to do so today unless granted an exemption for scientific purposes – but it is easy to visualise the way in which it might have worked.

Two men at either side of a net perhaps twenty or thirty yards across would probably be far enough apart to be on either side of a sitting covey. As they walked forward with a good length of net trailing behind, with or without the dog under it, they would presumably have clapped the net down into the heather as soon as the first grouse started to rise. Given very quick reactions they might net the bird as it rose, but

The Irish setter has a long history and is still one of the most popular pointing dogs for grouse shooting.

it is more likely that the net would capture those birds that were still crouching in the heather.

I can also see some practical difficulty with doing this, not least that the net would be constantly catching up and snagging on the heather stems, but it was once an established method of killing grouse. I can also see possible uses for it today as a means of capturing live grouse for relocation or in order to dose them with a wormer or even perhaps treat them for ticks if such a thing is practical. I have talked to a man who has practical experience of netting grouse and learned that the birds would sometimes stay crouched in the heather even after the net had been trailed above their hiding place, though when he first began experimenting he had supposed that the sight and sound of the net being dragged above them would have flushed them. Netting over a dog would be less likely to damage the birds than using a stake net. Kearton records that grouse flying at full speed with a good breeze behind them were often killed or badly injured when they struck the net.

Our subject though is grouse shooting, and it is to the early days of shooting that we must look next.

Firing a black powder muzzle-loader was, and still is, a smoky business.

It first became practical to shoot birds on the wing when the flintlock was developed. Briefly, a flintlock is a means of igniting the powder charge in a gun using sparks generated by striking a piece of steel with a chip of flint. In a flintlock action the flint is held in the jaws of a cock that is spring-propelled so as to hit a piece of steel called a hammer that rests on a priming pan containing a pinch of powder. The sparks ignite this powder, which then flashes through a touchhole to ignite the main powder charge inside the barrel of the gun, rifle or cannon. Somewhat confusingly the part known as a 'cock' in a flintlock action was later called the 'hammer' as percussion guns replaced those with flintlock actions.

The development of the flintlock meant that there was relatively little delay between the gunner pulling the trigger and the charge leaving the muzzle of the gun. (I use the word 'relatively' because later methods of ignition using percussion caps rather than flint and steel are noticeably faster.) Early guns were ignited by a slow match – in effect a smouldering piece of string – and while this was reasonably adequate when firing a cannon at an opposing army or a castle wall it was of little use when trying to get a shot off quickly and accurately enough to kill a grouse flying away from you at forty or fifty miles an hour. The flintlock though made it possible – though not easy – to kill birds on the wing, and with it brought about the conception of the modern sport of game shooting.

In the early days of sporting shooting – the latter part of the eighteenth century and the early years of the nineteenth – grouse were almost invariably shot over pointers and setters. Using a dog was the only practical way to find grouse during the early part of the season when the coveys will often sit so tightly that they won't rise even when someone walks right through the middle of them. In theory it would be possible to wander about the moor carrying your flintlock and shoot any grouse that you walked up, but in practice it would be an extremely inefficient way of shooting them. If they were sitting tightly it is unlikely that you would see more than a tiny fraction of the birds on your beat, whereas if they were in a flighty mood they would be liable to rise long before you were in range. A good team of pointers and setters would at least afford you the chance of making a decent bag.

Also, Georgian and Victorian sportsmen were accustomed to shooting over dogs. The main low ground quarry in those days was the grey partridge and though it was practical to walk up partridges with a line of guns many shots preferred to shoot them over pointers and setters. This might be for aesthetic reasons – there is a great deal of satisfaction to be gained simply from watching a good team of dogs in action, whether or not your intention is to kill partridge or grouse – but there could also be more selfish reasons for this preference. If you are one Gun in a line of ten then you might reasonably expect to get a shot at one tenth of the partridges that are flushed. If you are shooting on your own over a good team of birddogs you (or rather your dogs) can cover just as much ground as the line of ten Guns while allowing you to enjoy one hundred per cent of the shooting.

'Selfish' is perhaps the wrong term to apply in this case. Walking up and shooting over dogs are very different ways of achieving the same objective and many people (including me) would argue that shooting over dogs is a far more enjoyable way of spending a day than walking up as one of a line of Guns. Two hundred and fifty years ago sportsmen took great pride in their dogs, just as many of us do today, and no doubt took the same pleasure as we do from watching them work and enjoying the benefits of their skills.

Today shooting over dogs usually takes place on moors where there is a relatively low density of grouse, with the better moors being reserved primarily for driven grouse shooting. Our very rough rule of thumb when working our pointers and setters for shooting parties used to be that ten brace was a pretty good return for a day on the hill. We have done better than that on many occasions and, it must be said, there have been plenty of days when the bag has been nowhere near ten brace, but in general twenty grouse in the game bag at the end of the day will see everyone – Guns, dogs and handlers – happy.

Back in the nineteenth century though much bigger bags over dogs were common.

Shooting party with pointers to find the grouse and spaniels to retrieve the shot birds.

Fifty or a hundred brace per day was not unusual and in 1871 the Maharaja Duleep Singh shot 440 grouse over dogs in a single day. That particular day would have required a rather more robust organisation than we are used to today. The Maharaja had three brace of dogs working at the same time and rode from point to point on a pony. He must also have had a whole raft of dog handlers, boys to lead the spare dogs, people or ponies to carry the shot birds, more dogs to retrieve them, someone to supply him with spare cartridges, someone to hold the pony when he dismounted to shoot (unless he shot from the back of the pony) and no doubt someone to serve lunch at a suitable point in proceedings. Things are usually simpler and less labour intensive today.

My ideal shooting party for dogging would consist of two Guns, one dog handler, and a team of pointers or setters. To that we might add someone to lead the spare dogs and perhaps a Labrador or a spaniel to pick up the shot birds. If everyone was carrying a gamebag by the end of the day we would each have five grouse, assuming a ten brace day. Now five grouse in a gamebag is a very reasonable load to lug over the hill. If, on the other hand, we shot a hundred brace as the Victorians sometimes did, we would be carrying fifty birds apiece, and I can assure you that a man with that weight of game over his shoulder is not exactly going to skip lightly across the heather.

Of course the sportsmen in those far off days didn't burden themselves with industrial quantities of grouse. A pony with panniers could double up by carrying the lunch and supplies of powder and shot as well as acting as a mobile gamebag. Labour was also plentiful and cheap back then and there would have been no shortage of keepers, ghillies and boys to shoulder the load in the absence of a pony. I have worked dogs on a number of occasions with an Argocat – the modern equivalent of a hill pony – following along with lunches, spare clothing, extra cartridges and the like. While it is certainly convenient not to have to carry everything you might need plus everything you might shoot, I much prefer the more traditional beast of burden. The Argocat and the various other hill vehicles are undoubtedly a great help to stalkers and keepers everywhere, but they are also invariably noisy and intrusive, destroying the peace of the open hill and, more importantly, sometimes disturbing the grouse. On the odd occasions when we have been lucky enough to have a pony to bring out the lunches and take home the grouse the peace of the hill has been undisturbed and I am convinced the grouse sit better without the sound of an infernal combustion engine to alert them to our presence.

The change in fashion from shooting over dogs to shooting driven grouse took place from about the middle of the nineteenth century onwards. A number of factors combined to bring this about and the most important among them was undoubtedly the development of the breech-loading shotgun.

Grouse will often not flush until the pointing dog is almost on top of them.

Practically all early firearms from the great cannons used by the army and the navy to tiny pocket pistols carried for personal protection were muzzle-loaders. A gun in its simplest form need be no more than a tube sealed at one end and equipped with a small touchhole somewhere near the closed end. You load it by pouring first gunpowder and then some sort of projectile into the open end and you fire it by applying a spark or a flame to the touchhole. Then, if it doesn't blow up in your face, the bullet, shot, cannon ball or shell should come flying out of the muzzle bringing death and destruction to your enemy, his ship, his castle, his infantry and cavalry or possibly to a pheasant or a grouse.

Early firearms were set off using a slow match – essentially a smouldering piece of string – but over the years more efficient means of ignition were devised. The flintlock as described earlier held sway for many years but it was notoriously unreliable in wet weather because the powder in the firing pan would fail to ignite when damp. The invention of the percussion cap at the beginning of the nineteenth century introduced a more reliable means of ignition but initially guns were still loaded by pouring in powder and then shot and ramming them down with a ramrod. A highly trained infantryman at the time of the Napoleonic Wars could fire three or even four rounds a minute using pre-packed cartridges and not bothering too much about accuracy, but for the sportsman in the field quick reloading was not considered necessary.

One of the joys of shooting over pointing dogs is that the day can proceed at a leisurely pace. In the days of muzzle-loaders this was not just part of the pleasure, it was a necessity. Once you had fired both barrels (assuming that you were using a double-barrelled gun) you had to reload, and reloading was not something that could be hurried. Powder had to be poured down each barrel from your powder flask, then an over-powder wad rammed down, followed by a charge of shot from your shot-flask and then an over-shot wad, also tamped down with the ramrod. Then you had to put a pinch of powder into each priming pan or slot a percussion cap onto each nipple if you were operating a little later in the century. Slot the ramrod back into its loops under the barrels and only then were you ready to proceed. Time to reload? Probably not less than thirty to forty seconds – and that assumes that everything was ready to hand and that you weren't fumbling round in your pockets trying to find the right wads or the percussion caps.

The fact that it took a long time to reload fitted neatly with the fact that, before the invention of smokeless powder around 1870, firing a shot produced a cloud of smoke that effectively obscured the gunner's view for the next several seconds. On a still day, particularly when shooting grouse flying just above the ground, the second barrel may be effectively fired blind or require a swift sidestep in order to get a clear view of the remaining birds. The early breech-loaders were charged with black powder and this must have led to some very frustrating moments as grouse whipped past unseen through the fog of gun smoke. At least, with a muzzle-loader, the smoke would usually have dispersed long before the gun was ready to swing into action again.

Now half a minute may not sound very long but compare that with the two or three seconds that are all it takes to slip two cartridges into a modern breech-loading ejector. And then think how often, despite such rapid reloading, you have been struggling to get cartridges into your gun before the next pheasant sails high above or the next partridge slips through the line. Now imagine how long it would seem if you had to perform all the rigmarole of muzzle-loading while those birds were streaming past, unsaluted. Shooting with a muzzle-loader positively demanded plenty of time to spare between shots, and shooting over dogs made that time easily available.

Once birds had been pointed, flushed and (hopefully) shot, the dogs would (or should) drop into the heather and wait until the Guns had reloaded before going on to look for more birds. The command 'Hup!' still used by many handlers to order their dog to drop is supposedly a shortened version of the old cry of 'Muzzles up!' that told the other guns and the dog handlers that you were reloading and needed a break in activities to allow you to prepare for the next shot. Pointing dogs – if well trained – performed this function perfectly, dropping into the heather and staying put until ordered on to find the next covey, or quite possibly to point other birds from the same covey. Early season grouse often rise in ones and twos, and a well-trained dog could allow even the sportsman with a muzzle-loader the chance of having more than just two shots at a single covey.

But things changed for the better – or possibly for the worse, depending on your point of view, and back in the mid-nineteenth century there were some very solidly held points of view on this particular subject – with the development of the breech-loading shotgun. The modern shotgun evolved in the latter half of the nineteenth century and has changed very little since that time. By packaging powder, shot, wads and percussion cap in a cardboard, brass, or more recently, plastic tube and arranging for the barrels of the gun to hinge open at the rear end it became possible to reload a gun in a matter of seconds. This ability to reload rapidly had widespread implications in both the military and the sporting fields and brought about a revolution both in warfare and in the ways in which game shooting was organised and run.

Shooting with a muzzle-loader is of necessity a leisurely business. As we have already established it takes a considerable time to reload and the sportsman therefore needs the birds or animals that are his quarry to be persuaded to rise or run only when he is ready. The general pattern of shooting was to go out and hunt for game using either pointing or flushing dogs to get it out of cover and on foot or on the wing. Once a shot had been fired the dogs were dropped or the line held up while the guns were reloaded before moving on to find the next rabbit, partridge, snipe, grouse or whatever happened to be the quarry on the day. This situation might have continued even after the muzzle-loader was superseded but, at about the same time as the breech-loading shotgun became generally available, two other things happened that were, between them, to change the pattern of shooting forever. Man found ways to greatly increase the numbers of pheasants, partridges and grouse available to be shot and shooting became more fashionable among gentlemen of a more sedentary disposition.

In fact, there is no clear chain of cause and effect among the three elements. As far as the grouse was concerned better management of the heather and an often ruthless approach to predators had brought about a massive 'natural' increase in stocks, but pheasant and partridge numbers boomed because Victorian keepers and landowners actively sought artificial ways to increase numbers. The rearing field and the incubator made it possible for gamebirds (other than grouse) to increase far beyond the levels that could ever have been achieved by the birds nesting and rearing their chicks in the normal way. It is open to debate though whether the increased numbers came about because a means of rapid fire was now available, or whether the development of the breech-loader was hurried along because of the higher numbers of birds on the ground. Whatever the chronology, the almost inevitable outcome was the driven shoot.

There is no point in driving large numbers of birds over a line of Guns if the Guns are going to be spending fifty seconds out of every minute fumbling with powder flasks and ramrods and the other paraphernalia of the muzzle-loaders' art. Once a gun can be fired twice, then twice again a few seconds later, and again, and again, there will inevitably be those who prefer shooting to walking and who would rather stand at a peg while others arrange for the birds to come to them. Indeed, once game stocks reach a certain density driving can almost become a necessity rather than a choice.

A cocker spaniel retrieving a grouse.

Go into a wood containing a dozen pheasants and turn your spaniel loose. Given a good dog and reasonable luck you might get half a dozen shots. Some of the pheasants will sit tightly and be flushed within range, some will run and get up too far ahead and perhaps half of them will take to their wings at the sound of you shooting at one of the other birds. Now suppose there were five hundred pheasants in that same wood. Start the spaniel running, fire one or two shots and very nearly all those birds will be heading for somewhere more peaceful. You may still get half a dozen shots: in fact you will probably get more than that, but it is a fair bet that at least ninety-five per cent of the pheasants in the wood will leave without a shot being fired at them, either because they rise out of sight and out of range, or because they get up in a great cloud of clattering wings which means you can only shoot at two out of perhaps two hundred that are all in the air and in range at the same time. For the walking Gun, shooting over his dog, vast numbers of birds are not really a guarantee of vast amounts of sport.

But suppose that, instead of trying to shoot the birds as they rose in the wood a line of Guns were stationed outside the wood under the flight-path. By keeping the spaniel under close control and proceeding quietly (rather than firing a gun) it should be possible to get those five hundred pheasants up and over the guns a few at a time. And because the Guns can reload in a matter of seconds, they are going to shoot – or at the very least, shoot at – a fair proportion of the birds in the covert. The same principle applies to partridges and grouse. Given a big stock of birds, a well-organised beating line and a team of Guns with breech-loading weapons, far more birds can be shot than was ever possible or desirable when shooting in the old-fashioned way, walking in to where the birds were hiding and using dogs to point or flush them.

The third factor that helped to popularise driven shooting was the fact that not only could the driven Shot get a lot more shooting than his predecessor, but he could also do it with a lot less effort. He could be conveyed to his butt or his peg by pony and trap while his man followed along with his pair of guns in their oak and leather case, the cartridge magazine, the brace of retrievers, the canteen and whatever else was required. Lunch could be taken back in the dining hall of the great house, or served al fresco by uniformed servants if the weather was suitable. His man could stand beside him at the peg and load one gun while he was shooting with the other one, thus increasing his rate of fire still further. Teams of pickers-up could gather the birds at the end of the drive allowing the sportsman to go straight to the next drive without wasting any more time than necessary. In short, shooting could now be undertaken in relative comfort with fitness and stamina no longer being required in order to show off one's prowess with a gun.

Shooting became fashionable, with large comfortable lodges being built all over the Highlands and shooting parties being organised at the great houses in England. Where grouse shooting in its early days was often quite a rugged pursuit, with accommodation only being available in shepherds' huts and bothies or at rough country inns, by the end of the nineteenth century the sportsman could partake of his sport while still enjoying all the comforts of hot baths, roaring fires, five-course meals and comfortable beds. Lunch huts were built out on the more remote parts of the moors, and roads and tracks constructed so that the shooting parties could reach the butts with the minimum of effort. From a simple sport involving a couple of friends with their dogs wandering where their fancy might take them, grouse shooting evolved into something requiring a high degree of organisation, a host of keepers, beaters, flankers, loaders, pickers-up, pony men and quite possibly cooks, waiters and butlers to prepare and serve luncheon. The golden age of grouse shooting had arrived.

The coming of driven grouse shooting was not without its critics. It is human nature to resent change, particularly when the change involves something close to one's heart. The early Victorians prided themselves on their fitness and stamina; on their ability to walk all day long behind their dogs and to endure the hardships and discomfort that were often an integral part of a visit to the moors for shooting, stalking or fishing. Training a pointer or setter and bringing him on to the stage where he becomes a useful member of the team was (and is) a satisfying hobby on its own. Shooting over dogs sometimes requires more from the guns than just the ability to walk long distances over the heather and shoot straight when a target is presented. Real skill may be needed at times in the working of the dogs and in reading and understanding the terrain. For some Victorian sportsmen the notion that grouse could be shot, in considerable numbers, by someone who required nothing more than skill with a shotgun was an affront to the sport itself.

It must also be said that many sportsmen were unhappy when the percussion cap replaced the flintlock, when the breech-loader replaced the muzzle-loader and when the modern hammerless action took over from the old hammer guns. Telescopic sights on sporting rifles were scorned by many as making the sport too easy. I suspect that there may have been letters to the editor decrying the invention of snaphaunce and the flintlock and regretting the demise of the slow match. It is human nature for at least a proportion of the population to be suspicious of the new and to look back nostalgically to what it replaced, and field sportsmen are no exception. Indeed, it is arguable that those of us who shoot, fish, stalk and hunt are more wedded to tradition and custom than the majority of our peers.

In practice the advent of driven grouse shooting did not spell the end for shooting over dogs. Some sportsmen simply preferred the traditional way of doing things and carried on walking the hills behind their teams of pointers and setters. In some places driving the grouse was not a practical proposition, perhaps because the birds were not there in sufficient numbers to make driving worthwhile or because of local difficulties in recruiting enough beaters to shepherd the grouse over the butts. All that is strictly necessary to shoot grouse over dogs is one man, one gun and one dog and the decision to go shooting can be made at a moment's notice (and reversed just as quickly if the rain starts to fall). Particularly in the Highlands, where stalking and fishing were to hand as well as grouse shooting it was (and is) not unusual to wait to see what the weather looks like on the day before deciding whether to set forth with gun, rod or rifle.

Guns and loaders heading off on foot for the next drive.

A fine example of a double-barrelled shotgun – a design that has changed little over the past 150 years.

Organising a driven day means assembling beaters and a team of guns and normally has to be planned well in advance whether the beaters are recruited locally and come along on the day or are employed for a period of time and housed on the estate. Once twenty or thirty beaters, eight to ten guns, plus loaders, half a dozen pickers-up and four or five flankers are on parade the day has an impetus of its own and no longer lends itself to spur of the moment decisions as to whether to proceed or not. Certainly days will be washed out by rain or abandoned when mist swirls across the moor, but spontaneity is rarely a feature of the driven grouse shoot.

Driven grouse shooting and shooting over dogs are not mutually exclusive. There is no reason why both cannot take place on the same ground provided that the stocks of grouse are not too low for driving or too high for dogs to work satisfactorily. Indeed, shooting over dogs in the early weeks of the season when the birds are sitting tightly and then switching to driving a little later when the grouse have become wilder can work very satisfactorily to the benefit of both forms of sport. Shooting over dogs always becomes difficult later in the season when the birds are generally not prepared to sit tightly enough to allow a gun to come within range before flying off, but this very flightiness can be a boon to the keeper running a beating line. Coveys that are reluctant to take to the wing in August are easily missed altogether by a line of beaters spaced over a broad front, but later in the season those same birds may rise and sail over the guns with very little encouragement.

The golden age of grouse shooting referred to earlier can probably be considered to have lasted for about fifty years, from around 1860 to the outbreak of the First World War. There have been other great years since then of course, but overall grouse numbers have been subject to a slow decline ever since for various reasons that we have already considered – disease, forestry, destruction or fragmentation of moorlands, acid rain, global warming, ticks, heather beetle, predation, reduction in the number of keepers employed or whatever other cause you may care to blame. Possibly the great bags of the golden years were never sustainable anyway.

We may look back at some of the excesses of the Victorian era with a certain amount of disdain now and in the case of the great bags of pheasants made on some estates we probably do so with good reason. Producing vast numbers of birds and shooting thousands in a day brought great kudos to the landowners and keepers of the day, but is no longer considered acceptable by most sportsmen. Grouse however are something of a special case, since where nature – albeit with considerable help from man – produces a bumper crop of grouse it is not only desirable but positively necessary to make every effort to reduce numbers to a sustainable level before disease steps in to reduce them even further.

One of the difficulties faced by grouse moor owners in good years is to shoot the ground hard enough to stave off a crash the following year. This may sound like the sort of problem that every keeper and shoot manager would positively welcome, but in reality shooting enough birds in a really good season may prove an almost impossible task.

Once the grouse start to pack, shooting a reasonable proportion may become practically impossible. Huge packs of grouse crossing the butts look spectacular but the mathematics tell against the Guns and in favour of the grouse. If fifty birds sail over your butt in a single pack the very best that you can hope to do is to kill four of them – and that assumes that you are a) shooting with double guns, b) have a good, experienced loader to assist you, and c) are actually capable of killing four grouse with four shots. Even if you do, forty-six of the original fifty are still going to get away unscathed, and as the season goes on and the birds have been driven again and again it becomes more and more difficult to get them over the butts.

Some of the old records would not be looked on with favour if repeated these days. For example, in 1888 Lord Walsingham killed 1,070 grouse in a single day – a record that will probably never be beaten. He set out with the express intention of setting a record by shooting over a thousand grouse in the day and spent fourteen hours on the moor with many of the same birds being driven back and forth over him time after time. By the end of the twenty drives that made up the day I suspect that the surviving grouse, the beaters who put in twenty drives and probably Lord Walsingham himself were all exhausted.

From the end of the eighteenth century through the early years of the nineteenth grouse shooting was easily available to practically any gentleman who had the inclination to take part. The word 'gentleman' is used deliberately since prior to the Game Reform Bill of 1831 it was illegal for anyone other than a qualified landowner to shoot game. The 1831 Bill made access to shooting a little more democratic in that it allowed anyone to take part in game shooting provided that they had permission to shoot and that they held a Game Licence. The cost of the licence, which had to be renewed annually, was, of course, set well above the level that an ordinary working man could afford. Shooting was thus theoretically made available to everybody while still being restricted in practice to landowners and the relatively well off. The Bill also created a new offence of taking game without a licence to use against poachers.

As I write there is a proposal before Parliament to abolish the Game Licence. The current cost of £6 for a full season or £4 for a part season (July to October for grouse shooters or October to July for pheasant shooters) is hardly an impediment to anyone – peer or peasant – who wants to shoot grouse, partridges or pheasants and probably costs the government money for every licence issued. It is possibly the only item connected with shooting that has not risen enormously in cost over the past couple of centuries.

Grouse moors, particularly in Scotland, could be rented for what today seem like trivial sums. Ronald Eden lists some of the early rents in his fascinating book *Going To The Moors* (John Murray, 1979). Two moors on Faskally that were let for £8 in the 1830s were fetching £800 fifty years later, while Lord Malmesbury was offered the sporting rights on the island of Harris – including deer stalking, shooting and fishing – for £25 in 1833. Today £25 would just about buy you the right to shoot one pheasant on a commercial shoot and you would be lucky to find anywhere that offers grouse shooting

– driven or walked up – for such a trivial amount per bird. Of course, it must be remembered that £25 in the 1830s represented more than a full year's wages for many people.

In the early days of shooting grouse a great deal of shooting was available for nothing for the sportsman who had the time and the means to travel farther than the well-known moors. With vast areas of moorland available in Wales, the north of England and the Highlands and only a very few sportsmen wanting to shoot them there was little value in the grouse. Once improved transport facilities, primarily railways and steam ships, made access to the moors relatively easy more sportsmen began to take an interest in the grouse. Inevitably the law of supply and demand meant that buying or renting a grouse moor became more and more costly.

Despite the vast areas that existed in the nineteenth century, moorland was and is a finite resource. Pheasant shooting can be 'created' fairly easily by planting woodlands and using cover crops to create drives and rearing birds for release, and partridges thrive (or used to thrive) on farmland, but no such options are available where the grouse is

Beaters disembarking from their transport ready to start the first drive of the day.

Modern vehicles can bring the guns right to this lunch hut in the middle of the moors.

concerned. No heather moorland means no grouse, and heather moorland is not something that can be created in the same way that a new wood can be planted. For one thing heather and grouse need the proper type of moorland soil, for which read 'peat', in order to thrive, and most of the peatlands and uplands in Britain were already covered in heather. It is true that today there is a good bit of 'improved' grazing that can be converted back to heather moorland, but in the nineteenth century this process of liming, draining and re-seeding good heather in order to make poor grass had hardly started.

The second problem for anyone who might want to create a new habitat for grouse is the sheer scale of the area required. A new pheasant covert might take up no more than ten acres or so, but – even if it were possible to do it – a new grouse moor would be of little use if it covered less than perhaps a thousand acres. And even at a thousand acres it would need to be really good quality heather if it were to support enough grouse to make anything like a viable day shooting possible. If we leave aside those bits of moorland that were once heather and could become heather again given the chance, there is no realistic way in which a new grouse moor could be created today, and the same stricture applied a couple of hundred years ago. Grouse habitat is a finite resource, and once demand for shooting had grown enough to utilise all the moorland available it was inevitable that the cost of buying or renting a moor would rise, and keep on rising. And in the current era when grouse shooting is more often let by the day rather than by the season exactly the same model applies. If there isn't much of it, and there is no means of making more of it, then it will be expensive. And that applies to the red grouse just as it does to gold or diamonds or any other commodity that is in high demand linked to low supply.

The early years of the nineteenth century must have been wonderful for those few sportsmen who had the time, the means and the inclination to travel to the farther reaches of England and Scotland in search of grouse shooting. Grouse were plentiful, moorland was cheaply and even freely available, and there were few if any constraints on their sport. On the downside it should be noted that the available accommodation – if any was available - was often primitive, dirty, smoky, smelly and uncomfortable and the food was pretty much in keeping with the lodgings. Things certainly got better as the demand for grouse shooting increased, but they also got more expensive. Much, much more expensive.

In 1863 W. A. Adams paid £50 to lease a small moor in Aberdeenshire for three weeks' grouse shooting. He killed about thirty brace – a cost per bird of around sixteen shillings or eighty pence in today's money. Today you might well be asked to part with double the amount that Adams paid for the moor in order to shoot just one grouse. To be fair, Adams would have had to meet the cost of his keeper and dogs which, along with travel, accommodation and meals probably meant that the actual cost of his shooting may well have been as high as £2 per brace. It still looks quite reasonable when compared with the cost of shooting grouse today.

Adams though faced a long and hazardous journey to Aberdeenshire. The train would have taken about three days so he elected to go by paddle steamer from Scarborough to Aberdeen, then by train from Aberdeen to Gartly. Once there he stayed in what he described as 'plain but good enough' lodgings. Today you could make the same journey in a few hours by car or train or in even less time by aeroplane and have a choice of lodgings ranging from a simple bed and breakfast to a five star hotel. Adams shot all his grouse over dogs and you might elect to do the same, or to opt for driven grouse shooting always assuming that a sufficient stock of birds was available.

In that last respect grouse shooting has changed very little since the nineteenth century. The amount of sport that you will enjoy in any given season will depend entirely on how successful the grouse have been at nesting, hatching and rearing their young. Now, as then, good keeping and moor management can do a great deal to influence that outcome, but essentially, when you step out onto the moor in August, the prospects for the day and for the season depend on how well a population of completely wild birds have managed to find territories, pair off, mate, nest, lay, incubate and hatch their eggs, brood and rear their chicks and cope along the way with the weather, with predators, with disturbance and with whatever else Man and nature may

Gun and loader ready for action in a stone built butt topped off with turfs of heather.

throw at them. It doesn't matter whether you lived in the nineteenth century and paid less than a pound a bird to shoot grouse, or whether you are a modern sportsman paying a hundred times as much: grouse shooting is and hopefully will always be essentially about hunting a wild, free quarry on its own natural territory.

There may be less hardship to overcome in the twenty-first century, but the attraction remains the same. In the next chapter we will look at the ways in which grouse shooting is conducted today.

Grouse Shooting: Over Dogs

The single most important limiting factor in sporting shooting is that the maximum effective range of a shotgun is somewhere around fifty yards. How close to fifty yards will depend on a combination of the bore of the gun, the degree of choke in the barrels, the amount of shot you are firing and the size of that shot. Certainly you may be able to extend this slightly by utilising heavy shot loads, large shot sizes, tight chokes and big bores, but the laws of physics dictate that you will end up with either a very heavy gun or one that kicks like a mule, or even one that combines both of those undesirable attributes. Shooting live quarry with a shotgun therefore involves finding a solution to the fundamental problem of bringing gun and quarry to within less than fifty yards of each other. Once that has been achieved the onus moves on to the ability of the man behind the gun. Initially though he has to get within range of his quarry, and over the past two or three centuries he has devised a number of different ways of doing just that.

In general the sportsman either takes himself to the quarry or waits for the quarry to come to him, sometimes of its own volition and sometimes using the services of some form of outside agency. There used to be a third option whereby the quarry was brought to the sportsman and then released in order that he might shoot it but this practice has long been discontinued in Britain. I refer here of course to the sport of live pigeon shooting.

Gordon setter – a Scottish breed developed especially for long, hard days on the moors.

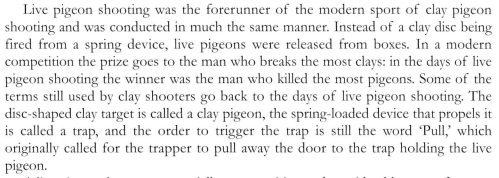

Live pigeon shooting was the forerunner of the modern sport of clay pigeon shooting and was conducted in much the same manner. Instead of a clay disc being fired from a spring device, live pigeons were released from boxes. In a modern competition the prize goes to the man who breaks the most clays: in the days of live pigeon shooting the winner was the man who killed the most pigeons. Some of the terms still used by clay shooters go back to the days of live pigeon shooting. The disc-shaped clay target is called a clay pigeon, the spring-loaded device that propels it is called a trap, and the order to trigger the trap is still the word 'Pull,' which originally called for the trapper to pull away the door to the trap holding the live pigeon.

A live pigeon shoot was essentially a competition and considerable sums of money could be at stake both as prizes and as side bets. Money was wagered both by the contestants and by spectators, the results were reported in the national newspapers and in 1900 at the Paris Olympics a Belgian, Leon de Lunden, won the only gold medal ever awarded for the event. I suspect that it is unlikely to make a return to the Olympic arena. It is still not uncommon to see advertisements for 'pigeon guns' in the shooting press and these refer not to guns designed for wood pigeon shooting, but to guns made specifically for the sport of live pigeon shooting. Generally they are relatively heavy guns that are tightly choked and designed to fire a large shot load because in live pigeon shooting a bird was counted as 'lost' if it did not fall within a designated distance from the gun. The live pigeon shot therefore needed a gun that would, as far as possible, guarantee a quick knockdown and a clean kill. A wounded bird that landed just outside the arc that denoted 'kill' or 'lost' could potentially lose the sportsman a great deal of money as well as his place in the competition.

It is also true to say that the requirement for a quick knockdown and a clean kill applies equally to any form of shooting involving a live quarry, but this does not mean that heavy shot loads and tight chokes are the best combination for the sporting shot. Those taking part in live pigeon shooting were not worried about damage to the carcase; their sole concern was to drop their birds inside the kill zone. Other forms of live quarry shooting make different demands on both the gun and the man behind it and while a heavy shot load and tight chokes may be ideal for some situations – very high pheasants for example – different types of live shooting and varying levels of skill with a shotgun mean that choosing the 'right' gun will depend on who is going to use it and for what type of shooting. One thing that we can be certain about though is that, in Britain at least, this will not include competitive live pigeon shooting.

But live pigeon shooting, even in its heyday, had little or nothing to do with sporting shooting where the essence of the sport is in hunting for one's quarry rather than having a live target released from captivity directly in front of your gun. There are a number of different approaches to the problem of getting gun and quarry into the same vicinity, though they can be broken down into three general categories. The gun can go to the quarry, he can wait in ambush for the quarry to come to him, or he can arrange for the quarry to be sent to him. Rough shooting over spaniels, shooting over pointing dogs, walking up and stalking all come into the first category where the shooter attempts to get himself within range of his quarry by going out and hunting for it. Flighting pigeons, waiting for wildfowl on the foreshore or shooting over decoys are the sort of things I have in mind that involve setting ambushes, and finally there is driven shooting where the normal procedure is for the gun to wait at a prearranged point while a team of beaters attempt to manoeuvre in such a way that the quarry will fly or run past within shotgun range.

As far as the red grouse is concerned though there are only three ways to go shooting. You can walk the birds up, shoot them over dogs (and please note that the two things are *not* the same) or you can drive them.

Although the quarry and the location stay the same whether you are driving, dogging or walking up, the three types of sport differ radically in the demands they make on the sportsman and on his equipment – his gun, ammunition, clothing and dogs. They will also have a varying impact on his bank balance with driven grouse likely to make the biggest hole in his wallet. Some of the requirements are absolute. If you want to shoot grouse over dogs then you absolutely must set out accompanied by a dog that will point grouse. You will not be able to shoot driven grouse unless you have someone to drive them for you. Other requirements come with a certain amount of flexibility. Almost any shotgun will serve for shooting grouse, be they driven, dogged or walked up. Certainly some guns will be more suitable than others. I would not care to carry a ten-bore fowling piece weighing the better part of a stone if I was walking up grouse, but it would serve the purpose if nothing else were available. And you might raise a few eyebrows if you took a pump-action repeater into your butt on some of the better class driving moors, but again; it would certainly kill grouse provided you pointed it in the right direction. In both cases though there are better choices to be made.

The same applies to your clothing, your dogs and the various accessories that accumulate around the sporting shot. For this reason I will devote this chapter and the next two to: shooting grouse over dogs, walking up grouse, and driven grouse shooting, and will consider each variation of grouse shooting individually with regard to the way the sport is organised and the clothing and equipment required. Obviously there are a number of items that are common to all three and a certain amount of cross-over, particularly between dogging and walking up where the need for boots and clothing suitable for walking over some possibly rough country are the same regardless of how you get your grouse on the wing. Conversely, some things are ideal for one form of shooting but not at all a good choice for another. For example, a very light gun that would be ideal for carrying about all day and firing relatively few shots while walking up might not be the most comfortable choice of weapon if you were fortunate enough to be stationed in a grouse butt with the prospect of firing a hundred or more shots in fairly rapid succession.

As with all types of shooting there are very few items that are absolutely essential – with the possible exception of the pointing dog mentioned earlier if you are planning to shoot over a dog plus a shotgun whatever your method of shooting. Even there you

The English setter is less common now than either the pointer or his cousin the Irish setter.

have considerable room for manoeuvre both in your choice of breed of dog and in the specification of your shotgun. You will also need some grouse of course, and permission to shoot them.

Since shooting over dogs was the original way of shooting grouse for sport we will begin there.

The first thing to establish is the meaning of the term 'over dogs' at least as far as this book is concerned. Shooting grouse over dogs means shooting them over pointing dogs; not over spaniels or Labradors or terriers or whatever other breed you might take out onto a grouse moor to help you get grouse on the wing. Shooting over dogs is shooting over pointing dogs, and if your dogs don't point then you are not shooting over dogs: you are walking up. This may sound pedantic – indeed, it may well be pedantic – but it is an important distinction where methods of grouse shooting are concerned.

The late Keith Erlandson regularly wrote letters to the shooting press taking issue with contributors and editors who mixed up the two forms of shooting. Keith, who was among the more outspoken and controversial of gundog trainers, handlers and writers, had little patience with those who wrote about 'walking up grouse over pointers' or described a walked up shoot as 'shooting over dogs'. In this he was quite correct and his reasons went further than simply wanting magazines to employ the correct termi-nology when publishing articles about shooting. Failing to understand properly the role of birddogs on a grouse moor can result in shooting being organised in a way that is inappropriate for both the dogs and the Guns. Pointing dogs have been bred over many years to work in a particular way, and running a pointer in front of a line of guns is not only bad for the dog but it can be dangerous to both the dog and the handler for reasons that will become clear later.

So since shooting over dogs means shooting over pointing dogs let us begin by establishing what we mean by 'pointing'. It is the action of a dog in stopping and standing motionless when he scents game and remaining still until ordered by his handler to get on and flush the birds. It is a natural part of the hunting behaviour of many predators to pause momentarily before seizing their prey. We can see this clearly in a hunting cat, creeping in until it is within springing distance of a mouse or a small bird, then freezing, motionless, but with every muscle poised to pounce. There must be some advantage in this behaviour from the point of hunting success, possibly that it allows the cat to build up tension in the muscles and concentrate its mind absolutely prior to the final rush in the way that modern athletes try to focus their concentration immediately prior to action. Certainly a cat about to pounce on prey is totally focussed on what it is about to do, and that same intensity of purpose can be seen in a dog when it is on point.

Cats hunt primarily by sight whereas gundogs rely much more on their noses and sense of smell to locate their prey. In this they differ from the gazehounds such as the greyhound, saluki, or lurcher that rely on seeing their prey in order to give chase. Bird-dogs, particularly young puppies, may sometimes be observed sight pointing at things as unlikely as butterflies or bees, but this behaviour is not pointing in the true sense of the word. Even though many adult dogs will come on to point at the *sight* of a grouse or a pheasant, sight pointing is not the purpose behind all those years of breeding. After all, if the dog can see the bird the chances are that the gun can see it as well, and once the gun can see his quarry there is no more need for a pointer. It is the ability of the pointing breeds to find game that is completely hidden from the eye simply by winding its scent on the breeze that makes them special.

In fairness, it is not only birddogs that will point. I have seen several Labradors for example that would come on to point momentarily before grabbing a wounded pheasant, partridge or grouse or before flushing game if they were being used in the beating line. These points are not usually particularly steady, nor will the object of the point generally be more than a few feet from the nose of the dog, but when a retriever or a spaniel 'points' in this manner it is simply exhibiting the same natural behaviour of its birddog cousins. In the latter though, centuries of selective breeding have honed the basic pointing instinct to the stage where it has become the main method for the dog to hunt rather than just a pause before flushing or grabbing the quarry.

For a dog to be any use as a birddog – and I use the term 'birddog' as a general catch-all for any of the pointing breeds – it must have a sufficiently 'long' nose to enable it to find game when still safely beyond the distance at which the quarry will choose flight over concealment, and it must be capable of holding its point for an indefinite

Champion Stake winning pointer Sparkfield Reason at work on the superb Bollihope moors.

amount of time. There are any number of other desirable characteristics that can be factored into the mix – pace, stamina and the ability to cover long distances over rough ground for example – but it is those two basic requirements that determine whether the dog is any good or not and, ultimately, whether you will be able to shoot grouse over him.

The principles of shooting grouse over dogs are simple. The dog is cast off and hunts the moor while the handler and guns amble along in his wake. When he finds grouse he points them. The Guns walk up to the point, the dog is sent in to flush the grouse and the guns shoot at the grouse. If so be as they shoot well there is a pause while the dead or wounded birds are collected, then the whole thing starts over again. This sequence of events continues until you have shot your bag, or run out of ground, run out of steam, run out of daylight, run out of grouse or run out of cartridges, until the dogs are too tired to run any more or until you simply decide to call it a day. Shooting over pointing dogs really is as simple as that. There are though a few small points that we ought to consider before setting out for a day over dogs.

I am going to qualify what I am writing with words like 'generally' or 'usually' quite a lot over the next few paragraphs. Any shooting day is likely to be a little bit unpredictable and grouse, being truly wild birds, are rather less predictable in their behaviour than partridges or pheasants that have been reared and released and are, to some extent, conditioned to react in particular ways to dogs, beaters and the like. Thus, while it is *generally* true to assert that grouse will sit tightly at the start of the season and become wild towards the latter part, every grouse keeper will be able to cite *specific* instances when birds have been wild in August but willing to sit tightly in December. This element of uncertainty is part of the appeal of grouse shooting.

In the early part of the nineteenth century shooting grouse over pointers and setters was the normal practice. Now, almost two hundred years later, the use of pointers, setters and HPR (hunt, point and retrieve) breeds on grouse moors is very much a minority sport when compared to driven grouse shooting. There are several possible reasons for this, some of which were outlined in the previous chapter. Driven grouse shooting can cater for teams of eight to ten Guns, involves far less physical effort on their part and is, arguably, the most exciting form of shooting to be found in Britain and possibly the rest of the world as well. It also generates considerable revenue for moor owners, attracts sportsmen from all over the world and makes an important contribution to the economy of some of the poorer rural areas of Scotland and northern England. Nevertheless, for a considerable number of Guns, shooting over dogs is still their preferred way of hunting grouse.

On many moors driving is simply not a practical proposition. Grouse numbers may not be high enough to provide sport for a line of Guns, nor to justify the expense of employing beaters and building butts. The terrain may be such that it is simply not possible to drive grouse so that they will cross a line of Guns. On some of the more remote Highland estates there would be very real difficulties in assembling enough beaters to drive the ground effectively even if there were enough grouse to make driving viable. And of course, there are still plenty of Guns who prefer the hard work of tramping the moors and hills to the relatively sedentary business of standing in a butt and waiting for grouse to come to them.

In general though, moors that carry a good stock of grouse will primarily be used for driven shooting, while ground where the birds are relatively scarce will be shot over dogs. Ten brace in the bag at the end of a day shooting over dogs should be enough to satisfy most Guns. Ten brace as the final tally at the end of a driven day would be more likely to see shooting abandoned for the rest of the season to preserve the remaining stock. Two Guns who have walked for six or seven hours, fired perhaps sixty cartridges between them and come home with ten brace will no doubt be more than satisfied with their day on the hill. Ten Guns who have stood and waited in butts for six or seven hours in order to fire sixty shots between them and end up with ten brace are unlikely to feel as pleased with events.

This division between driving and dogging is by no means absolute. Many driven moors also organise days shooting over dogs. These may be run on the more marginal ground or on areas where driving is difficult for reasons of terrain or access, but in many cases they take place over the same ground as the driven shoot. There is no reason why driving, dogging and walking up should not all take place on the same ground – though obviously not at the same time. Indeed, a few days over dogs in the early part of the season can be positively beneficial by giving the birds a bit of encouragement to fly when, a few days or weeks later, they see a beating line crossing the moor. A day or two shooting over dogs can also be useful by helping the owners to make an accurate assessment of the stock. Combining driving and shooting over dogs also adds a bit of variety to the season.

But let us concentrate first on shooting over dogs. Most dogging days are organised for the first few weeks of the season when the grouse should be sitting tightly. As a very general rule, shooting over pointers is straightforward in August and much of September, becomes somewhat trickier in October and can be extremely difficult during November and December. That said, I was once out with a team of pointers on the Twelfth of August in what seemed to be perfect conditions and found the grouse so jumpy that it was almost impossible to get close enough for a shot. And I have shot grouse over pointers in December on more than one occasion when they have been sitting as tightly as they normally do in August.

Seeing pointers and setters in action for the first time can come as a bit of a shock to Guns who are used to shooting over well-trained spaniels or Labradors. In normal rough shooting the aim is to get the dog to hunt close enough to the gun for any game that is flushed to get up within shotgun range and this means that effectively a spaniel should work within twenty or thirty yards maximum from the handler. To see a pointer being cast off and setting out for the far horizon at full speed – and a pointer or setter at full throttle is an impressive sight – might lead the uninitiated to conclude that any grouse that are on the moor will soon be chased off it. It is only when the dog comes onto point that the rules of the game become clear.

Gun, handler and field trial judge making their way in to a point during a field trial.

The whole reason why pointers and setters have been selectively bred over hundreds of years is so that they can do all the hard work of finding grouse or partridge, snipe or woodcock. Once they have found something to point the Guns should then be able to walk up to where the game is hiding in a relatively leisurely fashion, fully alert and ready to shoot when the birds fly. The whole point (if you will excuse the pun) of birddog work is to find game without flushing it. Since the dog does not flush the birds he can work much further away from the Guns than the twenty or thirty yards limit of a spaniel. A pointer can – and if he is working on a good big moor with not too many grouse very well may – work two or three hundred yards away from the Guns. It is not at all uncommon for the dog to be out of sight of the shooting party, particularly when working in among peat hags or over broken ground. With birddogs there is a clear division of labour - they find the game: you shoot it. There is no advantage in you trying to do their work for them. If you have a spaniel or a Labrador with you there may well be a clear disadvantage if you insist on letting your dog hunt instead of keeping him at heel. But more of that later. Let us start by looking at how a day shooting over pointers and setters is organised and run.

The personnel may vary considerably depending on where you are shooting. At its most basic all that is required is a pointer and a man with a gun: a more up-market situation might involve a team of pointers and setters complete with a handler to work them and a dog boy to lead the ones that were not working, a keeper to organise the day, a picker-up with a retriever or two, the Guns, a pony and pony man to bring out the lunches, carry the spare tackle and take the shot birds back to the game larder and possibly a few non-combatants in the guise of wives and girlfriends – though in these politically correct times I suppose I should really refer to them as 'significant others' or some such non-sexist claptrap. But you get the picture. Shooting over dogs can be a very basic affair or it can involve quite a large expedition.

We have already considered the basics of shooting over dogs, i.e. dog finds birds, Guns walk up and shoot them, but there is a little bit more to it than that. We will assume at the beginning that conditions are good and that the handler is working his dog into the wind. The dog – if he is any good – should be quartering the ground from side to side ahead of the handler, going out a hundred yards or more on one side, then turning and taking a cast a few yards forward before coming back, passing the handler and going out on the other side of the beat. When he finds birds he should stop and point. Until he does, the job of the shooting party is to stay behind the dog and the handler, walk along quietly, keeping any spare dogs under control, and enjoy watching the dog that is running do all the hard work.

When the dog points the handler will signal for two Guns to come forward. Their job is to come up to, and just past, where the dog is on point and then shoot the grouse when the dog goes in and flushes them. As soon as they have fired they should reload and remain alert while the handler gets the dog to 'clear the ground' – i.e. make sure that there are no more birds still tucked down into the heather that can be flushed to give the chance of another shot. Once the handler and the dog have decided that there are

Grouse to hand at a driven shoot, though this moor is also used for shooting over dogs at the start of the season.

no more birds to put up the shot birds can be collected before casting the dog off again and looking for the next covey. At least, that is how shooting over dogs works when everything happens in the 'classic' manner. Sometimes things are not quite so simple and we will look at some of those situations once we have considered the reasons why things are – or should be – organised in the manner outlined above.

It should be obvious why the dog and handler are out in front. If you go blundering along in front of the dog not only do you get in his way but also you are liable to flush any grouse that are sitting on your line of march. The dog will not be happy about this, nor will his handler. The need to proceed quietly should need no explanation. I don't mean that you have to creep along in total silence, but it is best to keep the noise down to a reasonable level. Grouse have ears as well as eyes, and even though they may sit to a dog it is often possible to flush them just by making a bit too much noise. But why do I advocate walking together rather than spreading out across the moor?

There are several reasons for this. The first is that quite often a running dog will tend to set the distance he goes out on either flank by the last person he passes on that side. If your party is spread out over a front of perhaps two hundred yards the dog may end up trying to cover far too much ground. If he then tries to keep in front of the line of guns by making longer and longer cuts forward at each end of the beat he may over-reach the ability of his nose and begin missing birds. Some Guns, particularly those with spaniels or retrievers of their own in tow, think that by walking in line behind the dog they will increase their chances of a shot by walking up any birds that the pointer has missed. To some extent this can become a self-fulfilling prophecy, especially if, as mentioned above, the dog is pushed into taking in too much ground on each cast.

A good birddog, working under favourable conditions, will miss very few birds, if any, provided that he is allowed to do his job without being pressured from behind or distracted by other dogs hunting about on 'his' beat. He should take his general line of travel from his handler, though always working across the wind, and this is much easier for the dog if the handler is easily distinguished from the rest of the shooting party by walking twenty or thirty yards ahead of them. While I am quite happy to walk ahead of a group of people who are ambling along behind me with empty guns, I most definitely do not want to be thirty yards ahead of a line of people with loaded guns who are hoping at any moment to take a snap shot at a grouse.

While no doubt you will argue that you would be well aware of where I was walking and would never fire a shot anywhere near me, I wonder if you could be quite so certain as regards the dog? A friend of mine had an Irish setter blinded by a careless shot from a Gun who insisted on 'walking up' grouse as the same time as shooting over dogs. A bird jumped, he shot at it and didn't see the setter in direct line of fire. It is all too easy to make this mistake. If you are walking along with an empty gun and watching the pointer or setter work you will not only be free from any worries about firing a dangerous shot but you will also be ready to get into position as soon as the dog comes onto point. If you are concentrating on the possibility that your spaniel may flush a grouse from under your feet and all primed for a quick shot when it happens you are not going to be watching the pointer. A grouse gets up; all your attention is on that bird, the gun comes up automatically and you don't even see the dog in line of fire ahead of you…. Just don't do it. If you want to walk up grouse then walk them up. But don't ask me or anybody else to run a birddog ahead of the line while you are doing it.

The usual etiquette to be followed when a dog comes onto point is for two Guns to go forward with the handler while the other Guns (if there are others) stay back and watch. Obviously where there are more than two Guns with the shooting party there needs to be some agreement about how the shooting is shared. If there were (say) six Guns, then they could split up into three pairs and take turn and turn about to go forward to each point. Alternatively, they could decide that each pair would have (say) thirty minutes at a time during which they would go to every point. Either system potentially has both some advantages and some disadvantages.

Taking turns to go to each point is probably the fairest way of distributing the shooting evenly around the Guns. However, there has to be a fairly clear definition of what constitutes a 'point'. What if the dog points a lark or a pipit? What if there are grouse but they get up too far ahead of the dog for the Guns to have a shot? Will that count as turn over, or will the two Guns currently 'on strike' go to the next point as well?

If you are working on a timed system this problem won't arise. Another one might though.

Grouse are not usually found evenly distributed across the moor. The first pair of Guns might go for their full half hour without seeing a grouse, then the second pair might have a dozen points during their allotted time. Do they then stick rigidly to the plan or do they turn round after having had five or six points and suggest that they swap places with the pair who have just had a blank run? It depends on the individuals involved of course, and perhaps on how well the keeper knows where grouse are liable to be found. You could just be getting into the good ground, in which case you might as well enjoy your full ration, or it could be that you will soon be back into a much less productive part of the moor. It is a value judgement that only you and your fellow Guns can make.

Taking turns by time rather than by the point has one advantage in that the Guns who are shooting at the moment should be ready to go forward as soon as the dog comes onto point. From the handlers' perspective it is at best annoying and at worst downright infuriating to see their dog come onto point and then have to wait while an interminable discussion goes on to decide which set of guns should be coming forward to shoot this time.

These discussions – and I have heard quite a few of them while simmering gently and hoping that the grouse wouldn't run or that the dog wouldn't decide to go in and flush them anyway – almost invariably involve Guns who are offering to waive their turn in favour of the others. I have never heard an argument where someone was insisting that it was *his* turn to go and shoot. The usual format is along the lines of either 'You haven't had much shooting…' or 'I've had plenty of shots already…', countered by 'But it's your turn…'. This can sometimes go on for quite some time. While I can appreciate the generosity behind the offer and the sporting desire to see that everyone gets a fair share of the shooting, I could appreciate them much better if agreement had been reached *before* my dog came on point

But let us assume that there are no discussions as to whose turn it is to shoot in the offing and that it is the turn of you and your shooting partner. You are walking quietly along a few yards behind the dog handler, a pointer or a setter (or a GSP, a Weimaraner or a vizsla if you prefer) is quartering the ground in front of you and quite suddenly he gets a whiff of something interesting in the heather ahead of him and he slams on to point. What happens now?

The first thing to remember is that, when it is your turn to shoot, you should be watching the dog and the handler so that you will be ready to go forward as soon as you are required. If you are watching the dog you will know that he is on point. If, as sometimes happens, the dog is out of sight of you, but in sight of the handler the usual signal to let you know that there is a point is for the handler to raise one arm into the air above his head. He will be hoping that you are sufficiently alert to see this signal, not standing around in a group discussing the state of the stock market or the price of cartridges. If you are a couple of hundred yards away and not paying attention the

Ramming the charge down the barrel of a percussion muzzle-loader.

handler is either going to have to shout at you – not recommended on the grounds of disturbing one or both of the dog and the grouse – or he is going to have to walk all the way back to you, tell you that the dog is on point, and then retrace his steps to where the dog is – or was. Stay awake, watch what is going on and be ready to go forward as soon as required. That way you will keep the dog and the handler happy and probably shoot a few more grouse into the bargain.

The handler will usually approach the dog directly with a gun on either side of him, about ten to fifteen yards away. If things go according to the classic picture of shooting over dogs the guns will keep advancing until they are a few yards ahead of the pointing dog, the handler will then send the dog in to flush the grouse and the covey will get up somewhere just ahead at which moment you will discover how easy, or possibly how difficult, it is to shoot them. And much of the time that is exactly how it happens. However, there are also those times when things are not quite so simple. The wind may be blowing across the beat or even from behind you; the grouse may be running ahead of the dog; the dog could be pointing a single outlier while the main part of the covey might be behind him or off to one side. Birds may be right under the dog's nose, or they may be fifty yards ahead of where he is pointing. Different scenarios require slightly different approaches and only experience can tell you how best to deal with any given situation.

The ideal shooting party – two Guns, one handler and a pointing dog: in this case a German wire-haired pointer.

Fortunately, even if you and your fellow Guns are complete novices at shooting over dogs, the dog handler should not be. He should also be experienced at 'reading' the dogs: knowing from their attitude and behaviour what the grouse are likely to be doing. This is far from an exact science of course but the more you work a dog the better you can become at interpreting his body language. A good handler will always try to ensure that his Guns are in the best possible position to make the most of their chances any time the dog is on point. As a Gun there are a couple of things that you can do to help him in this laudable aim.

The first thing is to listen to what the handler is telling you *and then do it!* This may sound like a statement of the blindingly obvious, but some Guns seem to have a natural talent for ignoring any advice offered despite much nodding of heads and assurances of 'Okay, yes, right, got that.' If the handler is waving his arm to indicate that he wants you to get forward, then get forward. If he is calling you closer in to the point then come closer. If he tells you to stay where you are, then stay there until told to move. There will be a reason for it, even if it is not immediately obvious. Since quietness is generally a virtue especially when close by a covey of grouse you should be on the lookout for non-verbal signals as well as listening to what the handler is saying. Don't give all your attention to the handler though: half an eye will be plenty because mostly what you are watching for is grouse getting up out of the heather in front of you.

The Gun is ready for the grouse to spring as this pointer works on the edge of a peat hag.

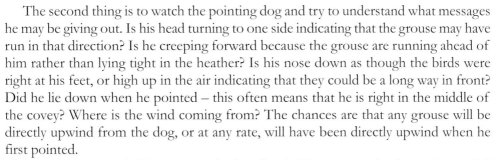

The second thing is to watch the pointing dog and try to understand what messages he may be giving out. Is his head turning to one side indicating that the grouse may have run in that direction? Is he creeping forward because the grouse are running ahead of him rather than lying tight in the heather? Is his nose down as though the birds were right at his feet, or high up in the air indicating that they could be a long way in front? Did he lie down when he pointed – this often means that he is right in the middle of the covey? Where is the wind coming from? The chances are that any grouse will be directly upwind from the dog, or at any rate, will have been directly upwind when he first pointed.

So now you have half an eye on the handler, half an eye on the dog and your full attention on any grouse that may jump out of the heather. It is actually a lot less complicated than it sounds. What I am trying to convey is that you should be aware of the dog, the handler and the empty space where you hope at any moment to see some grouse. Of these three things by far the most important is seeing the grouse when they rise.

A grouse bursting out of the heather seems to have the ability to go from stationary to full speed in the space of about three wing beats. Once up to speed he will very quickly be beyond the effective range of a shotgun. How much time you will have between your first sight or sound of him – and it is often the sound of grouse wings or the cry of the cock bird that will grab your attention even before your eyes have registered that he is there – will depend on how far in front of you he was when he got up. Which is why you should, whenever it is practical, try to be ahead of the pointing dog as he rodes in to flush the birds.

Just do the mathematics. Imagine the dog on point with the covey twenty-five yards ahead of him. You come up and stand ten yards behind him with your gun ready. The grouse run ten yards, then get up, cover another ten yards or so while you are registering their presence and bringing the gun up to your shoulder… By the time that you pull the trigger they are effectively out of range at some fifty-five yards ahead. Now start again but instead of standing keep going forward until you are ten yards in front of the dog. This time the grouse will be about thirty-five yards ahead as you fire, and at thirty-five yards you only have yourself to blame if you miss. It is always better to be too close than too far away. If the birds get up right under your feet you simply let them fly until they are what you judge to be a sporting distance. If they get up too far in front they will be out of range from the start and getting farther out of range with every beat of their wings.

Since there will usually be two Guns at each point we should give a little thought to what constitutes sporting behaviour when selecting a grouse to shoot. In a perfect world the birds would get up equidistant between the guns and fly directly away from them allowing each gun to select two birds from the covey that are clearly on his side, but in the real world they seldom do that. They may swing off to one side or the other, split up and go in different directions, get up in a big bunch or rise in ones and twos. There may only be a single bird or perhaps a pair rather than a whole covey. Deciding who shoots and at what is mainly a combination of good manners and common sense.

If you imagine a line running directly out from the pointing dog and splitting the ground in two then, as a general rule, any birds that are on your side of the line are yours, and any on the other side belong to your fellow Gun. Thus if a single grouse rises on the other side of the line you should leave it to your partner to shoot. If he manages to miss it with both barrels and it is still safely within range there is no reason why you should not then attempt to wipe his eye – unless your sporting instincts tell you that having survived two attempts on its life already the grouse deserves to be left in peace for the rest of the day. If your partner happens to hit the grouse without killing it and it looks as if it might fly away carrying some shot then you should do your best to kill it rather than risk leaving a wounded bird to suffer.

Much the same applies if a pair gets up rather than just a single. If they are clearly on one side or the other then it is good manners for the further away Gun to allow his partner at least the chance of a right and left. If they are about central then each Gun should take the bird that is nearer to his side. A decent sized covey obviously will give both Guns the chance to shoot unless they rise well off to one side so that they are out of range of one Gun or possibly in such a position that a shot would pose a risk to either the dog, the handler or the other Gun. There is always a risk that both Guns will select the same bird, especially when the covey is scattered out away from the Guns and the nearest one gets up somewhere centrally but this can be hard to avoid especially when the grouse are well out and require quick reflexes if you are to get a shot at all.

On the subject of reflexes, if you are one of those people who are quick to react and tend to get your shot off before your fellow Gun you may find that you are getting more than your fair share of the shooting, especially if there are a high proportion of singles and pairs rather than coveys. If so good manners would suggest that you hold back and allow him first crack from time to time. Grouse shooting isn't a competitive activity – unless of course you are a member of a shooting party where it is.

Some Guns like to inject a little bit of competition into their shooting and will quite blatantly poach their neighbours' birds (obviously I don't mean 'neighbours' as in the owners of the estate across the march where poaching would be a criminal offence). I mean the kind of friendly rivalry that sometimes exists between the Guns in a shoot where shooting a bird that is clearly going to your neighbour is accepted as a joke and reciprocated on the first occasion possible. It isn't my kind of shooting, but I can see how it can be amusing *provided all those involved think the same way*, and are all playing the same game. Then it is a bit of friendly rivalry. If just one Gun is shooting that way then he is a greedy b*st*rd and the sooner you stop 'enjoying' his company the better.

For most of us though our conduct at any kind of shoot should be governed by politeness, good manners and respect for our fellow Guns, for the beaters, dog handlers, keepers and indeed everyone else involved in providing or enjoying the day's sport, not forgetting the need to show proper respect for the quarry.

What to Wear

The question of what to wear when out shooting on the hill can be a little complicated for a number of reasons. British weather is notoriously fickle and nowhere more so than on the open and exposed acreages of hills and moors. A baking August morning can quickly turn into a cold, wet afternoon – or vice versa. There will be times when the most comfortable outfit would consist of a pair of shorts and a cotton shirt; times when you would feel the benefit of tweed breeks, shirt, tie, waiscoat and tweed jacket, and times when you really need a warm, waterproof coat, preferably with a hood, over-trousers and gloves. They may all occur on the same day.

The problem with shooting grouse over dogs, and with walking up grouse, is that you are probably going to have to carry everything you need along with you. This isn't always the case; as we have already seen there are shoots where an Argocat or a pony will be on hand to carry all your spare kit; but in probably the majority of cases you will be responsible for hauling along whatever you decide is required for your comfort during the course of the day. And don't forget that as well as clothing this may include your food, drink, gun, cartridges and whatever you happen to shoot. It pays to think carefully and choose wisely when outfitting for a day on the hill.

Dressed for the moors: good boots, gaiters, tweed breeks and a waterproof coat.

Whenever you are going out onto the hills and moors for whatever reason it is essential to check the weather forecast and really listen to what is said. Then take a good look at the day and use your own judgement and experience to balance what the official forecaster has just told you, and finally, and probably most importantly, ask the keeper what he thinks the day will do. Local knowledge is generally of far more value than the pronouncements of the London based experts, despite all the technology available to them. I have often been driving to work in a torrential downpour while Heather the Weather is twittering away on the radio to the effect that 'It is a lovely sunny start to the day right across the country…' Or, yet again, vice versa. In BBC terms 'the whole country' tends to mean the bit between Dover and the Wash, and you are unlikely to be shooting grouse anywhere there.

The first thing to bear in mind is that, whatever the weather, you will be walking several miles across country without benefit of any sort of track or footpath for most of the time. On some moors with relatively flat ground and well-burnt heather the going may be fairly easy while on others steep slopes, rocky crags, long heather, bogs, mires, peat hags, scree slopes, burns, rivers, cliffs and gullies may have to be navigated during the course of the day. You *will* need a good pair of boots.

At one time the choice of a boot for the hill was a simple one between wellies and tacketty boots and since the general advice was that rubber boots were not suitable for the hill, walking the hill meant getting a pair of what were usually described as 'stout leather boots' and spending a few days/weeks breaking them in – that is to say, getting the boots and your feet into a state where they were compatible. This involved many applications of oils and waxes (to the boots) and simultaneous applications of plasters and blister remedies (to the feet) before, finally, you felt able to walk any distance in them. Thankfully all that has changed now and there is a bewildering variety of footwear available for the hill walker at, it should be noted, a bewildering range of prices. So what do you need for a day on the hill walking up or shooting over dogs?

Only two things really matter: safety and comfort. Of these safety must be your first requirement and is primarily to do with the grip afforded by the soles of the boots with support for the ankles a secondary consideration. Your requirements will vary according to the type of ground you are going to have to walk over. On a nice, flat moor with a good access road you could probably walk all day in a pair of trainers. On a steep hillside those trainers might have so little grip that you would be in real danger of falling to your death. If you know for a fact that you will only be walking across flat, well-burnt heather and will never be shooting over any rougher, steeper ground, then your choice of boot will be less vital than if you are expecting to be tramping along the sides of a mountain. In either case though, you need a boot with a good, thick sole with a pattern of cleats that will ensure a firm grip on rock, peat, mud or heather – even heather can be quite slippery at times.

Comfort starts with having a boot that will not cause blistering on your heels and toes. Never go to the hill in a pair of boots that you are wearing for the first time because you will almost inevitably end up with the skin rubbed off some part of your

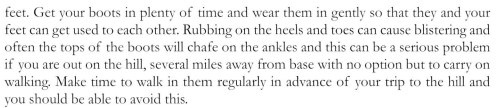

feet. Get your boots in plenty of time and wear them in gently so that they and your feet can get used to each other. Rubbing on the heels and toes can cause blistering and often the tops of the boots will chafe on the ankles and this can be a serious problem if you are out on the hill, several miles away from base with no option but to carry on walking. Make time to walk in them regularly in advance of your trip to the hill and you should be able to avoid this.

Never buy boots that are too tight, especially around the toes. If your big toe is butting up against the front of the boot it may be perfectly okay as long as you are walking on the flat, but once you start to go downhill you will be in very real discomfort. A toenail that has been subjected to a long assault from the front of a boot is liable to turn black and drop off – but only after inflicting a lot of pain on the owner. Boots shouldn't be so loose as to allow your feet to slip around inside them, but neither should they be so snug as to feel tight. When you are trying them on in the shop you should remember that you will be wearing thick socks inside them when you go to the hill, so either wear or borrow a pair of thick socks before making a purchase.

Although the old-fashioned rubber wellies were considered unsuitable for the hill – despite which, I have seen a good few professional stalkers and hill keepers who wore them quite happily – the modern Wellington boot comes in a number of guises, many of which are designed for just the sort of walking that you will be doing when you are shooting over dogs. It should also be noted that they are considerably more expensive than the good old welly that was the standard country wear for agricultural workers in past years. You can get rubber boots that are lined with leather or neoprene, that have proper grippy soles, have straps and zips to ensure that they fit properly around the calves and come in a range of tasteful colours to blend with the rest of your outfit. They will keep your feet dry as far as water coming in from the outside is concerned – provided the rubber is intact – but whatever they use for their lining they will make your feet sweat since rubber is impervious to moisture no matter whether it is incoming or outgoing. Provided that they have a good, grippy sole and give a measure of support to your ankles there is no reason why you should not wear rubber boots to the hill, though my own choice would always be for a proper walking boot rather than a welly – except for days when it is really, really wet.

Walking through wet heather presents the waterproofing on boots with a much sterner test than many of them are designed to handle. I have owned several pairs of boots that were alleged to be 'waterproof' and were so as far as normal wear was concerned. Rain didn't penetrate them and walking through puddles or even quite deep standing water was handled easily but a wet day on the hill was a different matter. The problem is that the heather is constantly rubbing against the boot as you walk and forcing the water into the fabric. If you are wearing leather boots then no matter what water-proofing concoction you have worked into the leather it will be rubbed off within the first mile or so. It is possible to get boots other than rubber Wellingtons that will keep your feet dry on the hill, but manufacturers' claims that they are 'waterproof' are often slightly overstated. If the label just says 'water resistant' then on a wet day you might

When shooting over dogs there is always time to stop for a rest and smoke.

as well dunk your feet in a bucket of water as soon as you put the boots on. It will give you more time to get used to the feeling of wet feet.

That said there are good, comfortable boots available that will really keep your feet dry all day whatever the weather as well as providing you with a firm grip. You are more likely to find a satisfactory pair by buying from a specialist shop where the staff know what they are selling and the kind of treatment the boots will be expected to suffer. A good fieldsports retailer or a store catering for the hill-walking and climbing fraternity should be able to discuss your requirements with at least some experience of moorland walking. Any of the magazines dealing with fieldsports will have advertisements from mail order retailers specialising in boots and other items of clothing suitable for the grouse moors and many also have websites for the computer literate among us. Perhaps the best way to source a decent and waterproof pair of boots is from the recommendation of someone who has a pair of their own and has tested them in all conditions – if you know anyone matching that description.

The cost of the boots may be a factor in your choice. If you are just having a day or two on the hill once a year or so then, provided your boots are safe and comfortable to wear, the fact that they will let your feet get wet under the worst conditions is

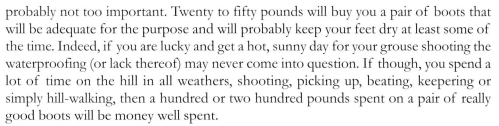

probably not too important. Twenty to fifty pounds will buy you a pair of boots that will be adequate for the purpose and will probably keep your feet dry at least some of the time. Indeed, if you are lucky and get a hot, sunny day for your grouse shooting the waterproofing (or lack thereof) may never come into question. If though, you spend a lot of time on the hill in all weathers, shooting, picking up, beating, keepering or simply hill-walking, then a hundred or two hundred pounds spent on a pair of really good boots will be money well spent.

Working our way upwards, the next thing to consider is your socks. The important thing is that they fit well, filling up the gap between your feet and your boots so that your feet won't slide around inside the boots – a sure recipe for blisters. Well-padded feet will soften the impact as you walk and the wool (or whatever else they are made from) should be soft and smooth: knots and ridges will quickly set up irritation as they rub against your feet. Some people like to wear two pairs of socks to increase the padding and insulation for their feet. If you do you must ensure that the inner pair won't slip down and bunch up under the soles of your feet. The usual arrangement is to put on a long pair first and a shorter pair second so that you can get at the short pair if they start to slip. The long ones will be held up with tape or string or woolly garters or whatever, but if the short ones are underneath and slip down you will have to remove the long ones and possibly your boots in order to reach them.

Heather leaves, seeds and twigs have an annoying habit of working their way in through the tops of your boots. A pair of gaiters will prevent this and will also help to keep your feet dry by stopping water trickling down your socks and into the tops of your boots. If you are shooting in the Highlands they will also keep the midges away from your legs and believe me, this is an absolutely vital consideration on still, muggy days when the little brutes will otherwise take up residence inside your socks. Gaiters come in canvas, leather, nylon and various patented 'breathable' fabrics. The cheapest are usually adequate and waterproof but do tend to make your legs sweat on warm days, more expensive makes should allow sweat to evaporate while still keeping the wet and the midges at bay.

The usual covering from the waist to the knees is a pair of tweed breeks and there is a lot to be said in their favour. Tweed stands up well to the rain and will keep you pretty much dry through light showers and drizzle and has the advantage of being warm when wet where some other materials seem to impart a chill to the wearer as soon as the first raindrops hit them. Other materials such as moleskin, corduroy, leather, loden cloth or cotton will also serve and there are a number of manufacturers producing waterproof trousers and breeks where the waterproofing is incorporated into the material. Full length trousers are okay but tend to get soggy around the calves and ankles when the weather is wet and the choice between breeks, plus twos and plus fours is one for the individual. The main thing is that whatever you wear is comfortable to wear and to walk in. Some Guns prefer shorts to breeks and provided that you have some means of keeping the midges at bay they are perfectly adequate – if you have the legs for them and are prepared to stand a little light ribbing from your friends.

Yellow Labrador with grouse. Using retrievers to collect shot birds gives the pointing dogs a break.

You will obviously be wearing a shirt, possibly with a tie and, depending on the day, a pullover for warmth. What goes on top of this can range from nothing, through sleeveless gilets and waistcoats, traditional tweed jackets to any of the numerous types of coat available for the field sportsman. The problem when selecting a coat is that it is impossible to know in advance whether the day will be cold and wet, befitting a tweed coat with waterproof lining, or hot and sunny and best tackled in shirtsleeve order. There is a strong possibility of course that both sets of conditions may prevail on the same day.

If you are fortunate enough to be accompanied by a pony with panniers, a quad bike and trailer or possibly an Argocat or something else of that ilk the problem may not exist since you can load whatever clothing takes your fancy into it and add or shed layers as the day demands. If though, you have to carry whatever you need with you,

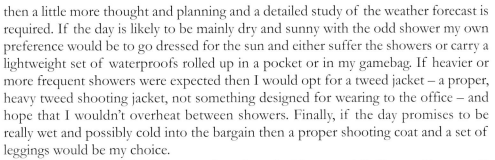

then a little more thought and planning and a detailed study of the weather forecast is required. If the day is likely to be mainly dry and sunny with the odd shower my own preference would be to go dressed for the sun and either suffer the showers or carry a lightweight set of waterproofs rolled up in a pocket or in my gamebag. If heavier or more frequent showers were expected then I would opt for a tweed jacket – a proper, heavy tweed shooting jacket, not something designed for wearing to the office – and hope that I wouldn't overheat between showers. Finally, if the day promises to be really wet and possibly cold into the bargain then a proper shooting coat and a set of leggings would be my choice.

On a warm day a light shower can be quite refreshing especially if a good breeze will dry you out soon afterwards. On a cold day getting wet can make you thoroughly miserable and put you at risk of hypothermia. That said, if you are burdened with a heavy coat on a hot day it will add nothing to your enjoyment, whether you wear it and sweat or drape it over your gamebag and suffer the weight of it dragging on your shoulder. If you already have one of the lightweight, fully insulated, totally waterproof and fully breathable type of coats then it will be ideal on most days, but if you don't you may baulk at spending several hundred pounds for one on the chance that you may need it on the one day a year you go grouse shooting. Unless of course you are out on the hill three times a week from August to November in which case you are a lucky man and any investment in warm, light dry clothing will be money well spent since you will reap the rewards on a regular basis.

For shooting over dogs or for walking up grouse the colour of your outfit is probably not important at least as far as the grouse are concerned. There are three different theories governing the look of your clothes when shooting over dogs. The first says you should wear typical shooting clothes with colours designed to blend in with the background and be as inconspicuous as possible so as not to spook the grouse. The second, as vouched for by a man who tended to wear white shirts when shooting over his dogs, says that grouse are more likely to sit tightly to an obvious threat since sitting tightly is their main defence in the early part of the season, therefore something bright and obvious is your best bet. The third theory – and the one that I favour – is that it probably doesn't matter at all since the grouse will sometimes sit and sometimes fly and what you are wearing won't make a shred of difference. The choice is yours.

Convention and courtesy would suggest that the sensible choice for breeks, jackets and coats is one that sees you clad in regular country sports colours and patterns. Going shooting wearing a Dayglo anorak might make no difference to the grouse but it will mark you down as someone who doesn't care for the normal 'rules' that govern shooting and may be perceived as showing a certain disdain for your host and the rest of the shooting party. Most of us prefer to fit in with the rest of the team rather than stand out as a non-conformist rebel and, possibly more importantly, most of the rest of the team will prefer it that way too. If you want to make a fashion statement on the hill you might like to consider some of the more eccentric designs of sock available or perhaps something colourful in the way of a tie.

A hat of some sort is useful for keeping the rain off your head, the sun out of your eyes and the midges out of your hair. Flat cap, deerstalker, baseball cap, trilby or Stetson: it doesn't really matter what you choose provided that it is something that will remain in contact with your head on windy days. If you elect for one of those broad brimmed cowboy type hats you should ensure that it is a good fit or add a lanyard so that it won't blow off and go bowling across the moor in a northerly direction when you are supposed to be heading south. A hat makes a lot of difference to the amount of heat you lose and can be invaluable on cold days. It is also useful if you can roll/fold it up and stuff it in your pocket or in the gamebag on those days when you are too hot – not something that can be done with a Stetson.

Other Equipment

One item that you really should take with you is a gamebag. Okay, you might not need it if there is the pony/Argocat that we have mentioned before to carry the grouse, but if not you will need some means of carrying what you shoot unless the keeper or the dog boy is marked for game hauling duties. You should not turn up bagless and assume that someone else will be available to carry things for you. Besides, a gamebag is useful for carrying your lunch, a flask or a bottle, perhaps your waterproofs, midge repellent, spare cartridges and whatever else you feel may come in handy during the day. A very large gamebag will hold a lot of tackle plus a lot of grouse, which may be advantageous when there are a lot of grouse to be shot. It also serves as an open invitation towards the end of a good day for your fellow guns to start wondering if you have 'any spare space in there…'.

As far as I am concerned a stick is almost essential when walking the hills and moors. It is a great aid to balance on steep ground or when wading through burns, it is handy to lean on when pausing for a rest and it is something to tie the dogs to when eating lunch. You don't need an expensive horn-handled crook, nor one of those high-tech, collapsible walking poles, since a length of ash or hazel cut from the hedge will suffice, but there is nothing wrong with something a bit more aesthetically pleasing either. The stick can be a nuisance when going in to the point since you either have to poke it into the ground and then go back for it later, hand it to one of the non-combatants to hold, or take it in with you and then remember to drop it as you bring the gun up to your shoulder. Attaching the stick to a lanyard would make sense as you could then let it trail behind you when you needed both hands free, though there is always the possibility that it might wedge in a rock or get caught in the heather just at the moment you were bringing the gun up to your shoulder.

A camera and/or a set of binoculars can add to your enjoyment of the day provided that you don't mind carrying them. The moors may look bleak and barren at first glance but there is always something to take the eye, from a skylark to a herd of red deer. You can often see for miles on the open hill and binoculars can turn a few vague bumps on the horizon into a bunch of stags or, distant speck in the sky into a soaring eagle.

If you are picking up on a dogging day a gamebag is essential to carry the shot birds.

They are also useful at times for following the flight of a pricked grouse and marking it down for retrieval. Pointing dogs are ideal subjects for the photographer since they stay in one place when on point and often strike spectacular poses. On a good day, with the heather in bloom, a blue sky and a background of distant mountains it is possible to take some superb pictures of dogs and Guns at work.

You could also include a small first-aid kit in your bag – a few plasters, midge repellent, some cream to soothe midge bites if the repellent doesn't work, maybe some sun block if you worry about that sort of thing. Spare laces for your boots, gloves, sunglasses, safety glasses, a knife, matches, dog lead, survival blanket, map and compass…You can make up your own list of 'useful' things that you will probably never use. Just remember that you are going to have to carry them, all day long, and that something that felt light at ten in the morning may have assumed a different aspect by four in the afternoon after being lugged for ten miles over rough country. And finally, if you really must take your mobile phone 'for emergencies' (and I can see where it might be useful if you fall and break a leg), then keep it switched off until your leg actually snaps.

Guns and Cartridges

For the majority of people going grouse shooting, whether over dogs, walked up or driven, the gun they will use is the gun that they already have, so in some ways trying to specify the ideal gun for the moors may be of little value. Most of you will not be buying a new gun especially for shooting grouse, though if you were looking for an excuse to add to your armoury then a forthcoming trip to the moors might serve. That said though, there are plenty of us who own more than one gun and plenty of guns fitted with multi-choke systems, so there may be choices to be made even if they don't include a visit to the gun maker with your cheque book in hand and your grouse gun specification scribbled on the back of an envelope.

If we are being absolutely honest when it comes to shooting grouse pretty much any gun will do at a push. You could set out armed with a four-ten or with a ten bore; with a twenty bore shooting a light load through open chokes or with a 3-inch magnum twelve bore choked full and full; with a best London side by side or a cheap Russian over and under, and provided you were within range for your particular combination of gun and ammunition, and provided you pointed it in the right direction, you would kill some grouse. Certainly some of these are better suited to grouse shooting than others, but all of them, plus any gun capable – in your hands – of striking a grouse with enough pellets retaining sufficient residual energy to kill it would be suitable for taking to the moor. Some though would be more suitable than others, for a variety of reasons, and in the next few paragraphs we will be examining those reasons in a bit more detail.

Let us begin by sketching out the requirements for a gun and a cartridge suitable for shooting either walked up grouse or grouse shot over dogs. What are the particular problems associated with this type of shooting? There are several, and in some cases taking the obvious solution to one problem will simply create another one. Let me try to explain.

If you are going shooting over dogs or walking up grouse you will not know until after you have set out whether the grouse will be sitting tightly and thus giving you a degree of control over the range at which you shoot them, or jumping wild and offering only snap shots at maximum range. Thus the gun that would be ideal when they are sitting tightly – something throwing a light shot load through fairly open bores – might be effectively useless when they were jumping forty yards ahead of you. Conversely, the gun that would cope with those grouse leaving the heather at maximum range – one chambered for magnum cartridges and bored full choke in both barrels – would have a tendency to smash any birds that you shot at a more modest distance.

Grouse on the wing are very quickly out of range of the Guns.

Whether you are shooting over dogs or walking up your grouse the majority of your shooting is likely to be at birds flying away from you. (There may be certain conditions when this is not the case as when, for example, you are working into the teeth of a gale and the grouse lifting ahead of you come swirling back with the wind under their tails.) In general though, you will be shooting under circumstances where the distance between you and the grouse is increasing with every beat of their wings, so a grouse that is too close at one moment will very shortly be at a more sporting range no matter what combination of gun and cartridge you are using. You can therefore regulate the range to suit your gun and cartridge combination simply by waiting until the grouse are at what you consider to be the right distance.

While the above might seem like a clear recommendation for tight chokes and heavy shot loads in practice this is not the case. A heavy shot load requires a heavy gun from which to fire it to keep the recoil within acceptable limits. The problem with using a heavy gun when shooting over dogs or walking up grouse is that you will have to carry that heavy gun all day long. The difference between a light twenty bore at five and a half pounds and a heavy twelve bore at seven and a half might not seem very much when you start out in the morning, but believe me, it will have made itself very clear by the time you have walked for six hours or so over hill and moor.

Excess weight is not the only drawback to using a heavy gun and shotload combination for grouse. In theory you can avoid ruining your grouse for the table by allowing them plenty of law before firing, but in so doing you will almost certainly reduce the number of grouse you shoot. Grouse are just the same as any other game bird in that the farther away they are the more challenging a target they present. Consider the pheasant by way of comparison. A reasonably sporting pheasant flying over your peg at perhaps thirty yards/ninety feet above you is eminently killable for the average shot. The same pheasant with an extra twenty yards of elevation putting it fifty yards/one hundred and fifty feet above the gun is going to sail away unscathed most of the time. It takes a real expert to kill pheasants at forty-five or fifty yards' range and most of us don't have that expertise.

Now a grouse is a considerably smaller bird than a pheasant. It will be flying almost as fast and will not afford you the luxury of watching it coming from a distant wood with plenty of time to calculate speed, elevation and required lead (though I fully accept that this is anything but an advantage for many shots). It will get up in a heart-stopping whirr of wings and at times require you to swing the gun and shoot almost by instinct if you are to get a shot off before it is out of range. You may be off-balance, stumbling over rocks or through long heather or teetering on the side of a hill, but you

If there is an Argocat to follow the shooting party it greatly reduces the amount you have to carry.

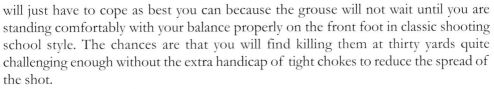

will just have to cope as best you can because the grouse will not wait until you are standing comfortably with your balance properly on the front foot in classic shooting school style. The chances are that you will find killing them at thirty yards quite challenging enough without the extra handicap of tight chokes to reduce the spread of the shot.

For some reason that I have never fully understood most Guns tend to over estimate the height of a pheasant but woefully under estimate the range of grouse. I was out on the hill a few years ago with a friend who was shooting over his own German pointer. For some reason he and his fellow Gun were a couple of hundred yards away on the other side of a valley and I was able to watch from side-on as the dog found and produced several grouse one after the other. In each case they were getting up well ahead of the dog and it was obvious that, by the time the Guns fired, the grouse were well out of shotgun range – at least seventy to eighty yards ahead. When we joined up again a little farther on both Guns were berating themselves for missing such a series of 'easy' shots.

This is far from uncommon even among experienced Guns. Estimating the distance from gun to grouse should be easy given that the birds are usually low enough to include the ground as a reference point, but in practice it can be quite tricky. It can sometimes be quite instructive to pace out the distance from shot to fall where the terrain allows it. You may find that you are not shooting quite as badly as you supposed.

A shotgun built on conventional lines will normally be choked tighter in one barrel than in the other and usually the placement of the triggers assumes that the more open barrel will be fired first with the choke following up for the second shot. While this may not be ideal when shooting driven birds it makes sense for shooting over dogs or walking up because the second shot is likely to be taken at a longer range than the first. This won't always be the case: sometimes the first bird to jump from the covey will be well ahead of the remainder: but as a general rule it will be correct.

It is often suggested that having an instant choice of choke available means that you can decide which barrel to fire first depending on whether the bird is close in or well out. In practice, particularly when snap shooting at grouse which have sprung out of the heather with no warning, most of us will instinctively fire the right barrel first (or whatever would be their 'normal' first barrel) rather than assessing the range and deciding that the choke barrel might be a better choice. Besides, if you do decide that the grouse is far enough out to justify the choke barrel and then either miss or just prick the bird your second shot – if you take one – will be through the more open bore – and how much sense does that make?

To sum up, a gun for shooting over dogs or for walking up grouse has to compromise between weight and range. A heavy gun firing heavy loads will clearly give you an advantage when the grouse are getting up on the limits of shotgun range, but it will handicap you when they are sitting tightly and, irrespective of the behaviour of the grouse, will have to be carried all day long. If you are shooting over dogs there are leather or webbing slings on the market that fit over the butt and the barrels to enable

Grouse shooting can bring you into some of the most beautiful country in Britain.

you to carry your shotgun slung from your shoulder like a rifle. There is no need to spoil the look of the gun by attaching swivels and some of these slings incorporate a means of quick-release so that you don't have to fiddle about with hooks or buckles every time a dog comes on point. They certainly ease the task of carrying your gun and leave both hands free to operate cameras and binoculars, sticks and dog leads, etc. If you are walking up grouse though you will simply have to carry the gun ready for a shot all day long.

The degree of choke in the barrels is very much a matter of personal choice if you have a choice in the matter. I suspect that the amount of choke in the barrels is only a minor factor for most shots when choosing a gun. It is a simple and relatively inexpensive matter to have the choke reduced in the barrels if they are bored tighter than you would like, though most of us, having acquired a new gun, are likely to use it and see how well they shoot with it before changing the chokes. If I were specifying a gun for shooting over dogs I would certainly want more choke in the left barrel than

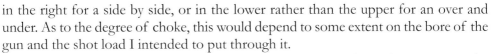
in the right for a side by side, or in the lower rather than the upper for an over and under. As to the degree of choke, this would depend to some extent on the bore of the gun and the shot load I intended to put through it.

With a small, light gun such as a twenty-eight or twenty bore there is a case for slightly tighter chokes than in a twelve bore because the smaller guns will normally be throwing a lighter shot load. There is though little point in trying to argue the merits of a gun bored ¼ and ¾ choke as against one bored ½ and full, or perhaps improved cylinder and ½ choke. Unless the gun has been individually regulated by an expert the actual amount of choke can vary considerably from the notional figure. In addition, the pattern thrown by the gun will vary according to the make, load and type of ammunition used. Felt wads will throw different patterns to plastic shot cups and the velocity generated by the propellant can also make a considerable difference to the end result. In practice much of this is irrelevant because most people going to the moor to shoot grouse are going to use their regular game gun irrespective of its bore, weight or degree of choke.

If you have a gun that you can shoot with a degree of confidence then use it and don't worry about whether it is the 'ideal' grouse gun. I have a twelve bore and a twenty bore in my gun cabinet at the time of writing and have used both of them to shoot grouse over dogs with about equal success. The twelve is bored ¾ and full choke, the twenty has improved cylinder in both barrels. In either case the gun will kill grouse if I point it in the right direction. When I miss – a not infrequent occurrence – the miss will invariably be down to operator error; not because the gun has too much choke or too little, nor because it is too heavy or too light.

If you have a choice of guns to take to the hill then I would suggest that a light gun will be better than a heavy one, but beyond that it is entirely up to you. As far as ammunition goes, size five or six shot would be the normal choice for grouse and personally I prefer felt wads (for all game shooting) so as not to scatter plastic shot cups all over the place. Pick up your empty cartridges whenever possible, though they may be hard to spot if you are using an ejector and they have been flung into some long heather.

You can carry your cartridges in a cartridge belt, in a bag or in your pockets. Most of the time you will be walking with an empty gun if you are shooting over dogs and with a loaded gun if walking up. The ability to reload quickly after firing is sometimes important because a covey of grouse will not always rise in a single bunch. Always reload as soon as you have fired your gun because there may be another chance of a shot at any moment. It helps therefore if you can get your hands on cartridges quickly without having to fumble open the buckle on your cartridge bag or unzip your coat to get at your cartridge belt. Keeping your cartridges in your coat pocket usually gives instant access to spare ammunition, but can be a problem in hot weather if you need to abandon the coat but then have nowhere to carry them. At least with a belt or bag you can march along in shirt sleeve order enjoying the sun while still having cartridges to hand. I would normally compromise when I was wearing a coat by having most of

Labrador bringing a grouse to hand through stalks of burnt heather.

my cartridges in a belt round my waist while keeping a few in my coat pocket ready for quick reloading. Then, if the sun came out and the coat went into the Argo I would just work from the belt.

The most important thing about shooting grouse over dogs (or any other form of shooting for that matter) is that you enjoy your day on the moor. If you are comfortably clothed and neither too warm nor too cold, can stay reasonably dry whatever the weather, are wearing boots that allow you to walk safely and comfortably across the heather and are not over-burdened with clutter; if you make an effort to understand and appreciate the way the dogs are working, listen to and follow the instructions given by the keeper and the dog handler and, finally, shoot a few grouse, then you should meet that criterion. If you don't, then you are probably following the wrong sport.

Grouse Shooting: Walked Up

e began the Chapter on 'Shooting Over Dogs' with a definition of the term, so it seems reasonable to do the same for walked up grouse shooting. Walking up means setting out across the moor, either alone or with anything up to a small army of fellow Guns and shooting at any grouse that rise from the heather in range of your gun. If you have a decent dog to work in front of you then you will most certainly shoot more grouse than if you are walking up without one. The essential difference between walking up and shooting over dogs as described in the previous chapter is that the dogs in this case will be flushing the grouse rather than pointing them.

As we have seen, grouse, particularly in the early part of the season, are usually reluctant to take to the wing unless there is clear and present danger, preferring to crouch in the heather and trust that you will walk past without seeing them – as you almost certainly will unless you have a dog to bustle them out for you. Many years ago when we were working on a shooting estate in the far north of Scotland one of a party of guests up for the salmon fishing in late July decided to arrive at the lodge on foot. To this end he had himself dropped off at the lonely Crask Inn and walked about eight miles across the hill and alongside the loch until he reached Loch Choire Lodge. One of his first remarks on arriving was that it was a pity that we had no grouse for the coming season.

Good retrieving dogs are essential if you are going to collect all the grouse that you shoot.

We had already been doing some grouse counts, mainly to get the pointers fit for the season, so we were a little surprised by this since all the signs were that we would be having an excellent year by our standards. There were grouse all over the estate, including the part where he had just walked for eight miles without seeing a single bird. The reason was, quite simply, that a man walking without a dog will often have to tramp right into the middle of a covey before they will rise, and the grouse has such superb camouflage that you will rarely spot them on the ground. Had it been the Twelfth or after and had he been carrying a gun it would have been a most disappointing walk, though I am sure that a decent spaniel hunting ahead of him would have put a few birds into the air. Later, shooting exclusively over pointers and GSPs we had some great days shooting including a couple of days on the very same ground that our guest thought was barren.

Sutherland, even thirty years ago when there were still a few grouse to be found in the far north, was never the most productive of areas especially when compared with the great driving moors further south. Even so, there is little doubt that our guest would have walked past quite a few coveys in the course of his trek and never suspected that they were there. I will grant you that it was late July, a couple of weeks before the shooting season, and that so far north the grouse are a little behind those in Northumberland or Yorkshire, so they would have been sitting tightly. But even if he had taken the same walk two or three weeks later I doubt if he would have seen many more – or even any more – grouse unless he had a dog to find them and get them on the wing for him.

As the season progresses the grouse tend to become more confident in their ability to escape predators by taking to their wings and the problem for the walking Gun changes completely. At the start of the season the birds may only fly when forced to do so by the close attention of a dog; later on they are liable to get up just at the sight and sound of a shooting party, often long before the Guns are anywhere near shotgun range. In between there are probably a few golden days when the birds will jump at exactly the right moment to allow a sporting shot. At least, I like to imagine that there might be, though I suppose the actual distance would depend on your ability with a gun and your definition of a sporting shot.

If you are shooting over dogs you will usually have ample warning before you are required to take a shot. Indeed, you will be, or should be, walking along with an empty gun and only slipping in cartridges when the dog is on point and you are walking in prepared for the flush. If you are walking up you have to be prepared to take a shot at any moment.

There will be times when you have a certain amount of warning that grouse may be about to rise. If you have a dog working in front of you and you are able to read his body language you should have a good idea when there are birds in the vicinity. You may hear grouse calling ahead or see them running. On wet days in particular the birds may sit with their heads up above the heather allowing the sharp-eyed to spot them. It is surprising how easily the head and neck of a grouse can catch the eye, especially if they are silhouetted against the sky on top of a ridge. Often when walking up birds will have been seen to drop in somewhere ahead of the line and obviously the guns will be more than usually alert when they reach the spot where the birds were marked down. This may – but will not necessarily – be the spot from which they get up again. Grouse often run as soon as they land and may be well away by the time you reach where they landed – or where you thought they landed which is not always the same spot.

Marking on the hill can be far more problematic than it might seem at first sight. The appearance of the moor from a couple of hundred yards away can be quite different from what you find when you have walked the intervening distance and are expecting to find your shot bird just on the edge of the peat hag, or lying beside the white rock that you had noted near where it fell. There may be lots of white rocks or peat hags that were invisible from your original perspective but which now present you with a bewildering array of possible sites for the covey or the shot bird to be lying. Even if you have marked the spot correctly the covey may have run after landing, as may the shot bird if it was not killed outright. It helps, where practical, to try to keep your eye on the exact spot where you have marked your birds until you are right up to it, but a dip in the ground may make this impossible.

Keeping in line is essential for safety and to maximise your chances of a shot.

Grouse can appear at any time. Often the first intimation that you will have that the chance of a shot may be imminent is the sound of a shot from somewhere else in the line. Grouse do not simply get up out of the heather and fly directly away from the Guns every time they are flushed. They *may* do just that and thus only offer a chance to one or two Guns directly behind where they rise, but they are just as likely to turn off to one side or the other and fly down the line or perhaps swing back over and present some of the Guns with a driven-type shot. Even birds that rise out of shot of the Guns further along the line may swing round sufficiently to offer a chance, particularly if there is a strong head wind, or if they are birds that have already been flushed once and moved away from their territories.

As with any form of shooting safety must be the most important consideration for anyone taking part. Walking up grouse can be a hazardous business for several reasons and it is important that everyone taking part is aware of the dangers and does everything possible to minimise the risk to themselves, the rest of the shooting party, their dogs and to anyone else who might be out on the hill.

Lightly dressed for the hill on a warm day and trusting that it won't rain later.

The most obvious source of danger is the simple fact that you are walking over rough ground and carrying a loaded gun. Trip or stumble, fall into a hidden drain, slip on some loose scree, tumble into a peat hag or simply lose your footing on a slope and there is always the possibility that your gun will go off inadvertently. You might snatch at the trigger as you react to the fall or the gun might go off of its own accord if it is bumped violently.

There exists among some shooting enthusiasts an irrational prejudice against hammer guns on the grounds that they are dangerous – or rather that they are more dangerous than a conventional hammerless gun. I believe that the reason behind this is that the hammers on a hammer gun are highly visible and, when pulled back to full cock, advertise the fact that the gun is ready to fire as soon as the triggers are pulled. What many Guns fail to realise though is that a 'hammerless' gun is actually not hammerless at all. The hammers (or tumblers) are simply concealed within the action. When using a hammer gun the action is only primed to fire when the hammers are drawn back into the full-cock position, and this has to be done by a conscious act of the shooter. A hammerless gun is cocked by the action of opening and closing the breech; therefore it is cocked at all times except when it has just been fired and the empty cartridges are still in the chambers.

As soon as the gun is opened the gun is returned to full-cock. Therefore, when you are walking up grouse (or indeed at any time when you have a loaded hammerless gun in your hands) the weapon will be at full-cock and ready to fire as soon as you pull the trigger – intentionally or inadvertently. This is the reason why most shoots insist on guns being carried with the breech open at all times except when you are expecting a shot. It is only by opening the barrels that it is possible to see with certainty that the gun is safe. Certainly, an empty gun cannot go off accidentally, but if the gun is closed then there is no way of knowing that it is empty. At least with a hammer gun – even a loaded hammer gun – there is practically no danger of it being fired accidentally as long as the hammers are in the down position, and if they are this is obvious for everyone to see.

That said, even if you are shooting with a hammer gun you should still carry it open and empty except when you are expecting a shot.

What virtually all hammerless guns do have – and it is something that most hammer guns lack – is some form of safety catch. This is a device that is designed to prevent the gun being fired inadvertently and normally takes the form of a button on top of the stock at the rear of the breech that has to be slid forward in order to allow the triggers to be pulled. When the safety catch is on the triggers are locked so that they cannot be pulled and, depending on the action of the gun, there will usually be some form of intercepting sear – a part of the lock that prevents the tumblers from striking the firing pins even if they are jerked loose by a fall or a blow to the action.

In theory therefore your hammerless shotgun should only ever go off when you have moved the safety catch to the fire position and pulled a trigger. In theory. In practice there is always the possibility – however slight – that a fall, or a sharp blow to any part of the gun might cause the tumblers to fall and fire the gun. Even with intercepting sears to provide backup to the trigger locks the gun could still go off unexpectedly. I have heard of an occasion when a shotgun fired both barrels as soon as the safety catch was slid to the fire position. Some form of knock had jerked the tumblers free only for them to be caught by the intercepting sears. Sliding the safety catch forward then released the tumblers and the man handling the gun got the shock of his life. (I am making some assumptions here as to the cause of the accidental discharge. If any firearms expert can provide me with a more accurate reason I would be interested to hear the proper explanation.) The fact is though, that a safety catch is not a guarantee against having a gun go off unexpectedly or as the result of a blow or a fall.

Unless you are a hammer gun fan, or even one of that happy band of enthusiasts who still shoot game with muzzle-loaders, the chances are that you will be carrying a normal, hammerless shotgun when you go walking up grouse. The point of the above few paragraphs is simply to emphasise the message that, as long as your gun is loaded, there will always be a danger – minimal though it may be – that if you fall or drop the gun for some reason it might just go bang without any help from your fingers on the triggers. And that could be serious or even fatal for you, your dog or possibly for the next Gun down the line.

If you want to walk up grouse it is a danger that can hardly be avoided. You will have to carry your gun loaded and ready for action since it is likely that at least some of the chances you get will only be possible if you can get a shot off almost as soon as you are aware that a grouse has risen. You must therefore be conscious at all times of where the muzzles of your gun are pointing and of where your next step is likely to take you. Even on a flat expanse of short heather there may be a rabbit hole, a hidden drain, a soft spot in the peat or an unseen rock to trip you up. On the wilder sort of moor just walking and staying upright may present a challenge. Carrying a stick can help with the staying upright part, but it may be a nuisance when that chance of a snap shot at a distant grouse presents itself. Good boots are also essential and it helps if you are experienced at walking on hill and moorland.

Keepers, shepherds and stalkers and others whose work takes them out onto the hill develop a knack of being able to watch their step at the same time as seeing what is happening around them. Anyone who has been out on the hill after red deer with a Highland stalker will have seen how he is apparently able to walk smoothly and easily over rough ground without stumbling or tripping while still seeing everything around him, from deer on a far off hillside to a skylark rising from the heather or the distant speck of an eagle soaring high overhead. In the meantime, you struggle along behind, stumbling over tussocks, turning an ankle on a rock and never seeing a sign of deer until they are carefully pointed out to you – and then only with the aid of your binoculars.

Only time and many miles of walking will instil this ability and the occasional stalker or grouse Shot just has to do their best to watch the ground under their feet as well as being ready to react at the first sign of a grouse. And, since you will be carrying a loaded gun, falling over is really not a good idea. As already suggested there is always the danger of the gun going off accidentally, but there is also the possibility that you might

Springer spaniels and a Labrador taking a break during a walked up shoot.

plug the barrels with peat or even break the gun. A gun stock is not designed to take the weight of a man falling across it and it is all too easy to snap the stock at the hand or to dent the barrels.

The risk of a fall when walking up is somewhat compounded by the fact that you have less discretion about your direction of travel than when you are shooting over dogs. In the latter case if you are confronted with a peat hag, a bog or a maze of shallow pools you can divert around them, but when walking up you have to maintain your station with regard to the rest of the line of Guns and as a result may find yourself tackling some ground that would be best left untrodden under normal circumstances. A certain amount of deviation is acceptable and even the most hard-hearted keeper will not expect you to wade through bog holes that come above your boots (and quite possibly above your waist…) but 'walking in line' means exactly what it says. You must walk in line with and (reasonably) evenly spaced from your fellow guns.

The principles of walking up grouse are simple. The guns and dogs, however many are available, line out across the moor and then set out in the direction of march indicated by the shoot captain, or keeper, or whoever is in charge of the day. The dogs work in front of the guns, the grouse get up, hopefully within shot, and the guns shoot at them. So far, so simple – but in practice, out on the hill, there are a few factors that may make things slightly less straightforward.

As we have already seen, shooting grouse when walking up in line may mean either taking snap shots or not shooting at all. When a grouse, or a covey of grouse, bursts out of the heather thirty yards or more away from you there are literally only seconds to register their presence, select a target, mount the gun and fire. If you were walking on your own there would be no problem about this – always assuming that you knew where your dog was when the birds got up – but when you are one of a line of Guns it is quite important that you know where you are in relation to your fellow Guns and to *all* the dogs that are working in front of your part of the line. Grouse have a tendency to fly close to the ground rather than springing into the air like pheasants, and there is a strong possibility that a careless shot might strike a dog or someone else walking in the line. Shooting one of your neighbours or one of their dogs is not considered what is now referred to as 'best practice'. Even if you miss, sending an ounce of shot whistling around someone's ears will not endear you to them and will probably result in any invitations to shoot in the future being withdrawn or immediate expulsion from the hill.

Gun suitably equipped for walking up with a well trained team of dogs.

The reason why it is so easy to fire a dangerous shot is that, when the grouse jump, there is not likely to be time for you to take stock of the situation around you, checking first right and then left to make certain of the location of both neighbours plus their dogs, your own dog and any other dogs that may have strayed away from their proper station before turning back to where the grouse got up. If you do, then the odds are that the grouse will be far out of shotgun range before you start to mount your gun. You need to be aware of where the dogs and your fellow Guns are at all times – as well as keeping alert for the first sight or sound of a grouse flushing and watching where you are placing your feet (see above). And you may well be climbing up or down a steep hill, deep in a peat hag, skirting around a bog hole or clambering through rocks as you go. Consider that the nearest guns may be sixty or eighty yards away on either side and the line could stretch across half a mile of heather and you will appreciate why walking up grouse is not quite as simple as, say, walking up partridges on a stubble field or pheasants in a root crop.

The most important thing from a safety point of view is for the line to *stay in line* and for individual Guns to neither race ahead nor lag behind. If you can be confident that the Guns are all properly in line at right angles to your direction of travel, then you can safely shoot forward through an arc of perhaps one hundred and twenty degrees, or turn round and enjoy roughly the same field of fire behind. You still have to watch out for any dogs in line of fire of course, particularly if you are firing down at grouse skimming low over the heather, but your fellow Guns should be safe. Unless you get a really unlucky ricochet off a rock….

Keeping a straight line while walking across the hill sounds simple in theory but can be a lot more difficult in practice. The terrain itself can cause problems in that one gun may have a clear expanse of well-burnt heather ahead of him while another is scrambling up a brae-face and a third is climbing in and out of a maze of peat hags or dodging around a series of boggy pools. Action – or a lack of it – can slow or stop part of the line. A dog may have hit upon the scent of a covey and be working away with its nose down in the heather trying to flush them while the Guns in the immediate vicinity have virtually stopped walking and are waiting for the first bird to jump. A shot bird falling behind may require a long pause while a dog completes the retrieve. Even birds that fall ahead may not be picked without stopping the line while time is spent searching the heather. While you are clearly not going to be able to maintain a line as rigid as a parade of guardsmen it is essential to keep an eye on your neighbours in particular and the rest of the line as well, as far as you can see them.

Ideally every one in the line will keep half an eye out for the rest of the Guns and their relative positions at all times so that slowing to allow those in rough ground to keep station happens automatically. In practice there may be times when the terrain prevents you from seeing the whole of the line, or even your immediate neighbours, and great care is needed to ensure that you do not fire a dangerous shot. If you do lose contact with the Guns on either side as you navigate peat hags or climb through steep ground it is essential to re-establish exactly where they, and you, are at the first opportunity.

So far we have been concerned with natural hazards to keeping a decent, straight line across the hill. There are also the vagaries of the Guns themselves to contend with and these generally fall into three categories. There are the hares who insist on pushing on ahead of everyone else; the tortoises who drop behind and the independent spirits who wander off without warning their fellow Guns. The last category often involves a Gun who has dropped a bird behind the line and goes back to collect it. Obviously every shot bird must be picked if possible, but dropping out of the line and going back is potentially dangerous for the Gun who does it, or who sends his dog back to collect the bird without alerting the Guns on either side.

If a grouse falls behind the line everyone should stop and wait until it has been picked and the Gun or dog picking it is back in their proper place. On a day when there are a lot of grouse falling behind the line this can mean an awful lot of stop/go progress and can be very frustrating for the Guns at the other end of the line, particularly if they are not getting much shooting, but safety must come first. A Gun or a dog fifty yards behind the line is in a very vulnerable position if more birds swing back through. In addition, if the line keeps moving while a Gun goes back to pick a bird it will take the gun quite some time to catch up again. This leaves a gap in the line where birds may be missed, or alternatively the Gun may lift them as he is catching up and find himself with a covey of grouse in the air with fellow Guns and their dogs directly in line of fire. If you have to go back, or send your dog back to collect a fallen bird then call 'Hold the line,' before you go and make sure that everyone has heard you.

While there is a good reason for going back to collect a shot bird the hares and the tortoises of the grouse moor are more annoying. While I have a certain amount of sympathy for the Gun who struggles to keep up there is no excuse for anyone to go racing off in front of the rest of the line.

I remember shooting grouse a few years ago with a man who was extremely fit and extremely proud of the fact and missed no opportunity to demonstrate his superior speed and stamina to anyone who cared to watch. We were shooting over pointers and despite all attempts to rein him in he insisted on galloping across the moor as if we were taking part in a foot race. At times he was even ahead of the dogs, never mind the rest of the Guns. It did mean that he got more than his fair share of shooting since he was invariably the first one to every point, sometimes even ahead of the dog handler. Instead of the handler and two Guns going in to the point together so that both would have the chance of a shot if the birds were jumpy, Mr Fitness was there first and on several occasions was the only one able to fire a shot. He certainly made an impression on me but I suspect it was not quite the one that he was hoping to make.

Pushing on ahead of a line of Guns is potentially dangerous, mainly to the person who pushes ahead, and may also deny the other Guns the chance of a shot that they would otherwise have had if the leading Gun pushes up birds that go forward. There is of course no need for such behaviour – anyone can go slowly across the hill.

Walking in line can be a real trial for the Gun who is struggling to keep up. If you are not fit enough to walk at a reasonable pace and for a reasonable distance then

Cocker spaniel eager to get to work hunting for grouse.

perhaps shooting walked up grouse is not the sport for you. Much depends on how you interpret the word 'reasonable', and how fit and active the rest of the Guns are. The keeper, or whoever is in charge of the line of Guns should try to ensure that the pace is slow enough to enable the least fit member to keep up. The other Guns should also try to set their pace so that the line stays in line, and where Guns are obviously struggling it makes sense to stop for regular breaks to let everyone get their breath.

Moving a little more slowly will not make much difference to the amount of ground you cover during the day and it may even be beneficial in that the dogs will be able to hunt the ground more thoroughly and perhaps find the odd covey that might otherwise have been missed. Most Guns will shoot better if they are relaxed and moving easily rather then panting and sweating from the effort of making a forced march over rough ground, and the day will certainly be more enjoyable if your lungs are not bursting and your eyes are not stinging with sweat. That said, the chances are that you will still end the day pretty well tired out. Walking the moors tends to have that effect on all but the fittest of sportsmen.

Never be afraid to call for a break if you are beginning to struggle. The odds are that at least some of the other Guns will be feeling the same way and may well bless you for taking the initiative. The dogs will benefit too and work better when they are refreshed.

Springer spaniels are ideal for flushing grouse for the Guns and retrieving them afterwards.

Having said that, you should not hold things up unnecessarily. I don't mind waiting while you have a breather, or pick a shot bird, or bring your dog in for a rest, but I prefer not to waste time waiting while you call your bookmaker on your mobile phone or get into a long discussion about share prices with your neighbouring Gun.

We have already touched on the need for dogs to find grouse, particularly early in the season. If you are walking up grouse your chances of success will be considerably enhanced if you have a good dog to work the heather in front of you. In fact, it doesn't even have to be a 'good' dog as long as it stays close by and hunts through the heather. The important thing is that it stays close. A dog that pulls sixty or seventy yards ahead and flushes birds is worse than no dog at all unless you are lucky and the grouse decide to fly back over your head. Pulling off to either side is less of a problem in that the dog may flush birds for your neighbouring Guns, which they at least will appreciate.

I would suggest that it is probably better to keep your dog at heel than to let him go racketing away in front if that is what he is liable to do. Even at heel if the scent is any good his demeanour should provide you with a warning that there are grouse about. That said, a good spaniel or retriever really working the heather in front of you is your best means of finding whatever grouse are on your part of the beat. Not only do the dogs find the birds for you but their body language will often tell you when the chance of a shot is imminent.

The question of noise from the line can be a tricky one to handle. If the grouse are at all jumpy the less noise that you make the better. However, keeping a dog close will often involve a fair amount of whistling and even the occasional shout, and staying in touch with the rest of the Guns may require a certain amount of raising of the voice. Certainly there will be calls to 'Hold the line,' and then more calls to move on again, not to mention the sound of shots. There is no need though to make any more noise than necessary. If you have something to say to one of the other Guns then wait until lunch to say it rather than bawling it across the heather. Even if the line is halted while someone picks a bird it is better not to have a conversation with your neighbour at the top of your voice. If you must talk then go across to him and talk quietly.

Before starting it is well to ensure that you know what may be shot and what should be left alone. Hares and blackgame are the two most likely species to feature alongside the red grouse as possible quarry and – assuming that you are shooting on or after 20 August when the black grouse season starts – you should check with your host whether or not they are included on the list of game that may be shot. Many shoots have imposed a voluntary ban on shooting black grouse, though on some moors there are still good enough stocks to allow a shootable surplus to be taken. Hares may be a questionable quarry for two reasons. Your host may want them to be preserved, or possibly, if there are young trees growing on the fringes of the moor, he may want them to be shot. The other thing to consider when a hare gets up ahead of you is whether you want to carry that hare for the rest of the day....

There may be rabbits and hares on the moor as well as grouse but check beforehand whether you are permitted to shoot ground game.

Snipe are also in season from 12 August and are often found on moorland particularly around wet, rushy areas. Rabbits would normally be considered fair game provided that you were willing to carry them and partridges may appear on the moorland edges. Again, it is as well to know in advance whether you are permitted to shoot them, always provided that 1 September has been reached and the close season has ended.

Clothing and Equipment

Although walking up grouse differs in certain fundamental ways from shooting grouse over dogs the clothing and equipment are very much the same. Both forms of shooting require clothes that will protect the wearer against whatever weather the moor may throw at him, be it rain, wind or baking sunshine. Good boots that will keep the feet dry, warm and comfortable are essential plus a careful study of the weather forecast before setting out. In one respect the walked up Shot is likely to be less well catered for than the man who is shooting over dogs, and that is the matter of auxiliary transport.

A ponyman or the driver of a quad bike or Argocat can easily follow along behind a party shooting over dogs and it is a simple matter to drop back and collect a spare coat, top up your cartridge belt, drop off a brace of shot birds or even hitch a lift if the day is proving too tiring. While there may be a pony or an Argo along with a walking up party in general it will not be so easily available. Unless the pony is led or the machine is driven right in line with the Guns it will have to hang well back for the safety reasons covered above. A line of ten Guns at fifty yard intervals will cover a front of just over a quarter of a mile and in practice the gap between the Guns may be considerably more than fifty yards. Nipping back to grab a coat could involve a round trip of half a mile or so while the rest of the Guns either stand and wait or carry on without you. And remember: if the line keeps advancing, while you are going a quarter of a mile back for your coat they will have advanced the better part of a quarter of a mile onwards, so now you have an even longer trek to get back into position.

If some sort of extra transport does follow the Guns or meet them at a prearranged point for lunch then you will be able to shed some of your burden at the start of the day – flask, sandwiches, spare cartridges perhaps – and then fill your stomach and your cartridge belt at lunch time. If not you are going to have to carry everything you need for the day, plus anything you shoot. Some form of compromise between comfort and convenience is clearly necessary. You may feel that it is worth while taking a bit more of a gamble on the weather than you would if you could pile a spare coat and a set of leggings into the Argocat. On a warm day getting wet from the odd shower may be preferable to sweating all day inside a heavy coat in order to stay dry when the rain comes. Equally, if it is cool and windy wearing the coat is likely to be better than getting soaked once and then shivering for the rest of the day. You have to decide, based on the weather forecast, a sensible appraisal of the feel of the day and how well you cope with being cold/wet/over-heated.

One item that you really should take along is a gamebag. Someone is going to have to carry whatever you shoot and unless you are very lucky that someone is going to be you. A decent sized bag is also useful for carrying things like your lunch, a flask of tea, extra cartridges, perhaps some lightweight waterproofs, midge repellent and any of the myriad other 'essentials' that you might want to take along. These might include (in no particular order) map, compass, global positioning system, camera, mobile phone, first-aid kit, snake bite kit for the dog, spare bootlaces, sunglasses, gloves, cartridge extractor, toilet paper, spare dog lead, survival blanket, corkscrew, matches and anything else that you think might come in useful *and that you are prepared to carry*. A couple of days on the hill are usually enough to see several items moved from the 'essential' category to 'not wanted on voyage'.

As far as your gun and ammunition goes the requirements are just about the same as for shooting over dogs. The majority of your shooting is likely to be at birds that rise at any distance from directly under your feet to the limit of shotgun range and often well beyond. As when shooting over dogs it is not the birds that rise too closely that cause problems since they can always be allowed to fly as far away as you consider sporting before you take a shot. It is birds that jump thirty-five to forty-five yards away that require some thought in the selection of a suitable gun and cartridge combination.

As long as you are walking and expecting, or at least hoping, to get a shot, you will be carrying your gun in the ready position. This may be across your forearm, over your shoulder, at high port with both hands holding it across your chest or at the trail, but always you must be ready to bring the gun up and fire a shot at the briefest of notice. Thus you cannot ease the weight of the gun by fixing it in a sling over your shoulder and I can assure you that even a light gun can feel heavy by the end of a long day's walking up. A pound or two of extra weight may not seem a lot but it can make a considerable difference over the length of a day. But, as we have already noted, a light gun normally fires a light load and will limit the range at which you might hope to kill grouse.

There is a further complication in that walking up grouse differs from shooting over dogs because the line of Guns tends to move birds further off their territories than the more local threat of a pointer or setter. Sometimes, having been pushed well ahead the coveys will get up and head back towards home and offer the guns the type of shot normally expected when driven shooting. If you are lucky enough to get into this situation you are likely to be better served by a more open bored gun than by one with full choke in both barrels.

Judging range on the moor can be difficult for many Guns and it is worth making the point that taking 'hopeful' shots at birds that are effectively out of normal range should be avoided. It is possible that you may pull off the odd 'miracle' shot and drop a bird dead seventy yards in front of you, but it is far more likely that a number of birds will be struck by the odd half-spent pellet and fly on to die slowly from the effects

of their wounds. Shooting at excessive range is unsporting, generally wasteful of cartridges and bad for the moor.

Getting the most out of a walked up day is mainly about working as a team with your fellow Guns. If you are on a moor with a good stock of birds you may all get a fair share of the shooting: on less well populated ground a walked up day can be much more of a lottery with some guns getting most of the sport while others may return in the evening with clean barrels. At least you can console yourself that you won't have been tiring yourself out carrying a heavy gamebag, unless you volunteer to take a few birds from one of the busier Guns. On some shoots the Guns draw for their positions in the line and stay that way all day, on other moors the line may be shuffled from time to time to bring the Guns from out on the flanks into the middle – though being in the centre of the line is no guarantee that you will be in the centre of the action. Switching positions around may also allow a little bit of social engineering and the Gun who insists on pushing ahead of the line can, with any luck, be sent to walk the steepest bits of the moor or take the outside edge when the line pivots.

A grouse collected from among rushes and long heather.

Labradors are primarily retrievers but can be used to flush grouse for the walking Gun as well.

A retriever that runs in and steals as many shot birds as it can from under the noses of the other Guns' dogs can be a real benefit on a busy shooting day. A benefit to the other Guns that is, because the owner of that retriever will end up carrying more than his fair share of the bag, which in some small measure may recompense for his dog's ill manners. Greedy shots are not usually a problem when walking up since your separation from your neighbouring Guns is normally far enough to preclude them shooting your birds. Grouse that are flying mid-distance between two Guns are another matter of course.

A day walking up can sometimes be frustrating, when birds are wild and rise out of shot, or when all the coveys are at the opposite end of the line, but you are pretty much guaranteed a good long walk over wild and beautiful country. Just being out on the moors is a privilege granted to only a tiny minority of sportsmen and even if there is not a lot of shooting, because you have to be ready for a shot at all times walking up keeps your mind alert and your nerves on edge throughout the day. It can provide sport for almost any number of Guns, where shooting over dogs is perhaps best conducted with only a couple. It is generally the cheapest form of grouse shooting – though bearing in mind the cost of shooting a grouse I should perhaps amend that to 'the least expensive' form – and probably the least efficient, which itself may be a good thing where the shootable surplus is small. Walking up grouse would be third on my list of favourite ways of grouse shooting, but it still rates a long, long way in front of a day in the office.

Grouse Shooting: Driven

Quite by coincidence I am beginning this section on driven grouse shooting on the Twelfth of August, which happens to fall on a Sunday this year meaning that there will be no grouse shooting until tomorrow. The past month has been a hectic one between grouse counting with the pointers, running a puppy in pointer and setter trials, releasing partridges and pheasants and, between times, trying to earn a living at the day job and with camera and word processor. Nevertheless I still try to make time to read a daily newspaper and as usual the opening day of the grouse shooting season is the subject of numerous articles and comment, some good and some risible.

Partly because of the attention of the media the British public have an awareness of 'the Twelfth' and its significance in the sporting calendar far beyond their knowledge of any other sporting dates. It is rare to see any comment made about the start of partridge and wildfowl shooting on the first of September and although the official opening of the pheasant season comes a month later pheasant shooting doesn't begin in earnest for several more weeks on most shoots and attracts no comment at all. But 'the glorious Twelfth' is firmly fixed in the minds of editors and writers and provokes an annual crop of stories in the papers, on television and on the radio, some of which may even contain a measure of truth.

Why so much interest in a sport that only involves a fraction of the number of people who shoot pheasants and is generally conducted far from the eyes of the general public? Partly I believe it is because grouse shooting evokes images of class and privilege: of tweed-suited aristocrats blazing away with expensive guns while humble peasants trudge the moors to drive the grouse over their butts and are expected to knuckle their foreheads and apologise for getting in the way if they happen to be struck by a careless shot. There is the occasional publicity-hungry chef or restaurant owner who sets himself a 'challenge' to have the first grouse of the season on his menu and hires a helicopter to fly a brace of birds in from the moor. And there are the attempts by those who do understand the sport to try to counter some of the more fanciful outpourings of the tabloid press by running serious articles about the economic benefits of good moorland management. Whatever the reason, the one date in the shooting calendar that has any significance whatsoever for the vast majority of the British populace is the Twelfth of August.

Beaters led by the keeper set out along a hill road to the start of a drive.

It is considerably easier to understand why grouse shooting is important to the parties actually involved. Driven grouse shooting is arguably the finest shooting to be found anywhere in the world. I suspect that most of those who might disagree with that statement would do so only because I included the word 'arguably'. For many sportsmen there is nothing but nothing to equal shooting driven grouse. While my own preference is for shooting over pointing dogs even I will gladly concede that this simpler form of sport cannot match the excitement of crouching in a butt and seeing the fleeting brown dots of an oncoming covey swooping and wheeling across the heather and then, suddenly, whistling through the line while guns crack, the smell of powder smoke assails the nostrils and a single feather drifting on the breeze is all that remains to say that the birds were ever there. There may be a better way to spend an August day but I cannot easily bring it to mind.

It is not just the quality of the shooting that makes the grouse special. The season opens in August and offers at least the possibility that you will be shooting under a blazing summer sun. The wild moorland scenery is particularly spectacular when the

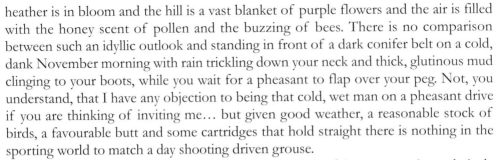

heather is in bloom and the hill is a vast blanket of purple flowers and the air is filled with the honey scent of pollen and the buzzing of bees. There is no comparison between such an idyllic outlook and standing in front of a dark conifer belt on a cold, dank November morning with rain trickling down your neck and thick, glutinous mud clinging to your boots, while you wait for a pheasant to flap over your peg. Not, you understand, that I have any objection to being that cold, wet man on a pheasant drive if you are thinking of inviting me… but given good weather, a reasonable stock of birds, a favourable butt and some cartridges that hold straight there is nothing in the sporting world to match a day shooting driven grouse.

From the point of view of the Guns, shooting the driven grouse is a relatively sedentary sport when compared to shooting over dogs or walking up. On many moors there will be roads leading right up to the butts so that the Guns can be driven out in a motor vehicle, dropped off exactly at their place in the line and have to walk no more than a few steps for each drive. On other moors there may be a stiff walk up the hill, particularly if you have drawn a number at the far end of the line, but in general the Guns stand and shoot leaving the walking and the responsibility for getting the birds within range to the beating line and the flankers, of whom more later.

In principle therefore shooting driven grouse is not unlike shooting driven pheasants. In practice there are a great many differences. For a start the grouse is a much more accomplished flier than the pheasant. A pheasant can only fly for a very limited length of time before it has to resort to gliding on set wings with just the occasional flap to maintain height and direction. In general, once a pheasant has set a course it is pretty much committed to that course but a grouse is far more manoeuvrable and can twist and turn or swing back on itself at will. The pheasant is like a heavy bomber compared to which the grouse is very much the equivalent of a fighter. A pheasant will be temporarily exhausted after quite a short flight and may not be physically capable of taking to the air for some time after landing whereas a grouse can fly, land and then take off again with ease.

Because of their limitations in flight pheasants are normally flushed quite close to the line of Guns (though they may have been encouraged to walk quite a way before being flushed). Grouse drives can bring in several miles of moor and require great skill on the part of the keeper if all the birds are not to go back or leak out of the sides of the drive. The grouse may fly forward from the beating line, drop into the heather and then rise and fly on again before crossing the butts. When they do reach the butts they are unlikely to be high in the air as driven pheasants should be, but rather skimming the contours of the ground. And where shooting a low flapping pheasant is hardly a challenge for a competent shot, a low grouse is something completely different.

On a driven pheasant shoot Guns and beaters will necessarily be working in quite close proximity for much of the day simply because of the pheasants' limitations of flight. On a driven grouse moor the beaters may start out a mile or more from the butts and only be visible to the Guns right at the end of each drive. They will also be extremely vulnerable over the last few hundred yards of each drive being directly in

The beaters closing up as they approach the butts at the end of a drive.

the line of fire. Indeed, grouse shooting is by some way the most dangerous of the various shooting sports practised in Britain at least as far as the possibility of one of the participants getting shot is concerned.

It takes a great deal of skill and experience to be able to drive grouse over a line of butts. A grouse that lives a completely free and wild existence out on the moors can fly in any direction that it chooses when it is disturbed by a line of beaters. There is no release pen to attract it back 'home'. There are no convenient woods to offer refuge: just miles and miles of heather any acre of which is apparently as attractive to a fleeing grouse as any other acre. Once on the wing the birds can go forwards or backwards, left or right, with the wind, across it or against it. Only years of experience and understanding of the way that the birds tend to behave under particular conditions of wind and weather enable them to be driven at all.

On one moor close to my home, the beaters start out well to the right of the line of butts driving the moor directly *away* from where the Guns are waiting. Eventually the line wheels through one hundred and eighty degrees, pivoting on the left-hand man, and then starts back towards the butts. The grouse – if they have read the script – will have flown forwards and left of the original line of march and will then be gathered up again and sent forward to cross the butts. At least, that is the way the beat is driven under normal wind conditions. Given an adverse wind a completely different approach has to be taken. It may even be necessary to send the Guns to a different line of butts and work the beat in the opposite direction. As a very experienced grouse keeper once told me, the most important thing for him to do on the morning of a shooting day is to get an accurate weather forecast, especially as regards the wind direction and strength.

Not all beats present such problems, nor require complicated manoeuvres from the beating line. Some drives are straightforward and simply require the beaters to start at point A and work directly towards the butts at B. On other beats bits may have to be blanked in from the sides to push birds across before sweeping them on in the direction of the Guns. There may be a series of drives aimed at both putting birds over the Guns and also gathering a reservoir of birds on a particular part of the moor to form the basis of another drive later in the day. The only way to know what will work and what will not work is through experience and local knowledge passed down through generations of moorland keepers.

One thing in the favour of the keeper is that grouse do tend, with inevitable exceptions, to follow roughly the same flight lines year after year, provided that

Lightly dressed on a warm day but with waterproofs ready in the belt bag.

conditions on the ground have not changed significantly. This is just as well since grouse butts tend to be permanent structures and do not allow the moorland shoot manager the same flexibility in placing his guns as is available on low ground shoots. We will look in more detail at the art of driving grouse in a later chapter. For the moment let us concentrate on what is required in order to take part in a driven grouse day as one of the Guns.

A grouse spends its entire life as a potential victim, vulnerable to predators in the air and on the ground from egg to adult. Living most of their lives in the lonely isolation of the hills and moors they are rightly suspicious of humans as well as of the smaller predators and don't take well to sudden changes in their surroundings. In trying to fly them over a line of Guns the keeper relies on the danger posed by the oncoming beaters to get them on the wing and moving in the right direction and then on flankers equipped with flags to turn them if they try to slide out of the edges of the drive. If the Guns simply stood on the heather in full view the chances are that the grouse, or most of the grouse, would simply fly around them. The purpose of a grouse butt is to hide the Guns so that the birds do not see them until they are committed to their line of flight.

In the early days of driving grouse the Guns tended to hide themselves in peat hags and natural gullies. Once a pattern of flight lines became apparent the practice of building permanent butts began and on many moors the butts in use today will have been serving their purpose for well over a hundred years. Since the butts are there all year round the grouse accept them as part of the landscape. A Gun, or perhaps a Gun and a loader, provided that they are sensibly dressed, keeping low and not moving about excessively represent little change in the scenery and therefore little potential danger in the grouse's eyes.

A grouse butt can vary from a simple wooden hurdle to an elaborately crafted, dry stone walled work of art. It may be sunken in the ground or raised up on stilts, built of wood, stone, corrugated iron or simply from sods dug from the surrounding peat. Some butts are so beautifully disguised that they are all but invisible from just a few yards away, though it must also be said that others may stand out as ugly eyesores across an otherwise pristine landscape. What matters though, aesthetics aside, is not what they look like to the Guns, but what they look like to the grouse.

Provided that the birds are familiar with those sheets of corrugated iron, scruffy heaps of turf, wooden hurdles, stone walled stells or sunken pits, and provided that the butt will mostly conceal the Gun from an oncoming grouse, they should serve their purpose. That said, the pleasure to be gained from a shooting day is made up of a whole series of little details, and there is no doubt that being in a well-built stone butt with fresh turves of heather on the top of the wall and a dry, level floor will feel better than crouching behind an old pallet stinking of creosote. However, it must also be recognised that given the choice between shooting one brace of grouse from the first butt and twenty brace from the latter most Guns would elect to put up with those creosote fumes.

The butts will usually be numbered and there will often be more butts than there are Guns to occupy them. This is to give the shoot some flexibility in placing the Guns according to the wind direction and any other variables that may influence the way the birds fly. Thus, given eight Guns and a line of twelve butts, the Gun who draws number one might be placed in butt five with the rest of the line occupying numbers six to twelve on one drive, with the occupied butts being switched to numbers one to eight if the next drive was being done in the opposite direction – an additional complication for those who find the concept of memorising a single number and then adding two to it before each drive too complicated for their brains to grasp.

It is always a good idea to listen to the shoot organiser and follow instructions and never more so than when out on a grouse moor where it is not always as easy to follow events as at a low-ground shoot. If you are asked to move smartly between drives then it is as well to do so or you may find yourself gossiping with your neighbour while the best birds of the drive – perhaps the only birds of the drive – whistle over your unoccupied butt. The beaters may still be a line of specks in the far distance but that doesn't mean that there will be no grouse on the move.

Once in the butt the first thing to do is to check your safe lines of fire. Unless you happen to be at one end of the line there will be another butt on either side of you, almost certainly within shotgun range. If you fire a dangerous shot from a grouse butt there is a very real danger of killing or blinding a fellow Gun, loader, beater or flanker – and it is very, very easy to fire that dangerous shot. You may not even be aware that you have done so until you hear the cry of 'Who fired that shot?' and by then it is far too late.

Good, safe gun handling. The Gun takes a shot in front…

... then elevates the muzzles as he turns...

... and takes another grouse behind the line.

The problem is that grouse fly low and they twist and swerve as they fly. On a pheasant shoot you will normally have clear blue sky (or perhaps dark grey cloud) around your target and can shoot with absolute confidence that only the pheasant is in any danger. On a grouse moor you will often be shooting parallel to the ground and even downwards at times and the danger to anyone within range is obvious.

Probably the greatest risk is to the Guns on either side of your butt. The cardinal sin of the driven grouse shoot is to swing through the line. The problem is that it is all too easy to do it.

Grouse tend to curve and turn as they fly in any case and when they suddenly realise that the butts are not empty as usual but bristling with men and guns they can jink and twist like fighter aircraft under attack. Birds can come at you suddenly, almost seeming to burst from the heather and will not simply hold course as they reach the Guns. They may lift or drop, swerve to either side, half turn and fly along the line of Guns or simply stream straight through between the butts. Birds that were out in front and appeared to be coming right down your throat may slide off to one side while others may suddenly flash into view as they jink away from your neighbours. In the excitement and the heat of the moment it is all too easy to lose your bearings and continue to follow a bird with the muzzles as it sweeps between you and the next-door butt. All your attention is on the bird and you won't even see the butt in the background until too late.

It is not just the Guns in the neighbouring butts that are at risk. Even if the grouse are well above the head of your neighbour there will be other Guns further down the line who will not take kindly to being sprayed with shot even if it is just about spent. Even at a couple of hundred yards a stray shot can still give a nasty sting. So don't swing through the line whatever happens. There may be assistance supplied to help prevent you doing this. Some butts have a couple of short sticks shoved into the top of the structure on either side to stop you from swinging the gun round at head height. Some moors actually erect physical barriers between each pair of butts so that even if a careless shot is fired the potential victims are protected. Ideally you will be shooting most of your grouse in front of the butt anyway, but if you must turn round with a loaded gun to take a shot behind you should dismount the gun from your shoulder and point the muzzles straight up in the air as you turn.

There are the beaters to consider as well. If you are shooting your birds ahead of the butt then you will quite likely be shooting towards the advancing line of beaters. While they are well out from the butts there is little danger for them since spent shot can patter down with no more impact than a shower of rain, but as they get nearer the situation becomes steadily more dangerous for them. The normal practice on most moors is for a horn or a whistle to be sounded towards the end of each drive to signal to the Guns that there will be no more shooting forwards. Any grouse that come after the signal must be allowed to pass through the line of butts before a shot is fired.

Turning round to fire behind the butt does not automatically mean that you have a completely free field of fire because there will probably be pickers-up stationed there

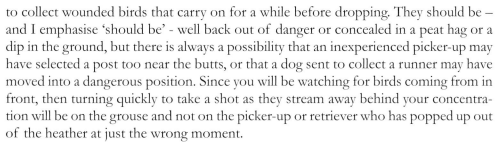

to collect wounded birds that carry on for a while before dropping. They should be – and I emphasise 'should be' - well back out of danger or concealed in a peat hag or a dip in the ground, but there is always a possibility that an inexperienced picker-up may have selected a post too near the butts, or that a dog sent to collect a runner may have moved into a dangerous position. Since you will be watching for birds coming from in front, then turning quickly to take a shot as they stream away behind your concentration will be on the grouse and not on the picker-up or retriever who has popped up out of the heather at just the wrong moment.

Never assume that a shot will be safe just because you haven't heard the horn that orders you to stop shooting forwards, or haven't seen any sign of a picker-up behind your butt. A beater or one of the beating dogs may have pulled ahead of the rest of the line; you may simply not have heard the horn when it was sounded; a picker-up may have come along from a neighbouring position and taken up station behind your butt while you were not looking. Concentrate on the grouse certainly, but make every effort to be aware of what is happening around you at the same time.

Besides your fellow Guns, the beaters and the pickers-up there may also be flankers stationed within shotgun range, particularly if you have drawn a butt at one end or other of the line. Incidentally, 'shotgun range' in this instance doesn't mean the distance at which a gun might reasonably be expected to kill a grouse – say fifty yards or so – but the distance at which a human or a dog being peppered with shot would be at risk of pain and injury to their person. I am not aware of any research into this matter, and I suppose it would in any case depend on the size of shot being used and perhaps the pain threshold of the person on the receiving end, but I would suggest that, up to perhaps two hundred yards, a pellet could cause a nasty sting and might do some real damage if it caught you in the eye.

The flankers' job is to attempt to turn any grouse that look like heading out of the side of the drive and send them back onto a line that will take them over the butts. The general principle is to stay out of sight until the opportune moment then pop up out of the heather and wave a flag at the oncoming covey. Surprise and fright should cause the birds to swing back onto the proper course. Flanking is sometimes an extremely skilful task with timing being critical to its success. It should be clear though that 'popping up out of the heather' just as a covey of grouse is passing might be a recipe for disaster if the covey were between the flanker and one of the Guns and close enough to the Gun for him to consider a shot.

If the day is properly organised the Guns in the end butts will have been warned in very clear fashion if there are flankers anywhere near their positions, but once again, it is never wise to assume that because you haven't been warned of a possible danger that the danger does not exist. If in doubt ask; and any time that you find yourself drawn in the end butt it is worth checking whether or not there will be a flanker anywhere close by.

After all that you may be wondering whether it will be possible for you to fire a shot at all for fear of injuring someone, be it beater, flanker, picker-up or neighbouring Gun.

Flankers with flags at the ready to prevent grouse from slipping out of the side of the drive.

Not to forget the loaders, anyone who has come along to watch the shooting, stray hikers, dogs and anyone else who can claim legitimate business in line of fire. In practice, provided that you have taken careful stock of your bearings with regard to the rest of the Guns, checked whether any flankers are concealed within range of your gun and made sure that you don't shoot forwards after the horn has sounded you should be able to relax and enjoy the sport. Though you may find it a little difficult to relax when you are waiting for the first covey to come skimming across the heather on the first day of a new shooting season.

'Waiting' may well be an accurate description of what you will be doing when you first get into your butt at the start of each drive. A grouse drive can involve bringing in vast acreages of moor – or certainly vast acreages when compared to the amount of ground covered on a typical low-ground drive – and there is an inevitable bit of 'hurry

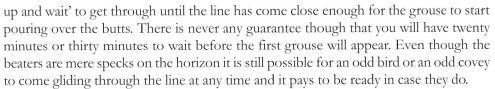

up and wait' to get through until the line has come close enough for the grouse to start pouring over the butts. There is never any guarantee though that you will have twenty minutes or thirty minutes to wait before the first grouse will appear. Even though the beaters are mere specks on the horizon it is still possible for an odd bird or an odd covey to come gliding through the line at any time and it pays to be ready in case they do.

You *may* hear the cock bird calling as the covey approaches the Guns, but they may come in complete silence. You *may* be able to spot them well out and watch them as they skim across the heather towards you, but they may cast up without warning from a dip in the ground and be over you before you have time to react unless you were holding yourself in readiness with gun loaded and in hand. It may be tiring to hold yourself in a state of constant readiness rather then relaxing, smoking a cigarette and having a chat with your loader/neighbouring Gun/significant other or whoever else may be within earshot, but if you turn your back on the drive and ground arms you will always run the risk of missing a chance. And who knows? It may be the best chance or even the only chance that you will get during the whole drive.

So be ready for a shot from the moment you get into position and keep at least half an eye on what is happening out across the heather in front of you – always supposing that you can see any distance in front. Quite often the butts will be built below the line of a ridge so that your view forward is restricted to just a few yards and any grouse that do come will only be in sight for a few seconds before they have whistled past.

A well concealed sunken butt with a dry, level floor.

Building butts in gullies and dips in the ground makes good sense as far as deceiving the grouse goes since there is no danger of them spotting the heads of the occupants from well out and turning away from the Guns. In many cases, unless they are flying well above the ground, the birds will actually be in shot from the moment they come into view. It follows of course that they will only be in shot in front of the butt for a very brief period of time.

If you are the type of Gun who shoots best when there is no time to think this can be a real advantage. There is a blur of movement above the heather, and there is a covey of grouse bursting into sight just fifty yards in front of you and closing the gap at what seems like a hundred miles an hour. All you can do is throw the gun up and snap off two cartridges with no time to think about gun mounting, or forward allowance, or proper footwork or anything at all except getting those two shots off as quickly as possible. It is snapshooting of the highest quality and – if you are a Gun who has quick reactions and the ability to shoot accurately without conscious thought – it can bring excellent results. Of course, if you like to see your birds well out and take your time selecting a target, mount the gun deliberately, swing through the bird with fine judgement of the lead required before pulling the trigger you are going to struggle – or take most of your birds behind the line as they are going away.

Butts built like these in a gully mean that snap shooting will be the order of the day.

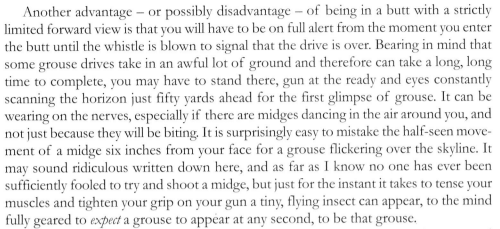

Another advantage – or possibly disadvantage – of being in a butt with a strictly limited forward view is that you will have to be on full alert from the moment you enter the butt until the whistle is blown to signal that the drive is over. Bearing in mind that some grouse drives take in an awful lot of ground and therefore can take a long, long time to complete, you may have to stand there, gun at the ready and eyes constantly scanning the horizon just fifty yards ahead for the first glimpse of grouse. It can be wearing on the nerves, especially if there are midges dancing in the air around you, and not just because they will be biting. It is surprisingly easy to mistake the half-seen movement of a midge six inches from your face for a grouse flickering over the skyline. It may sound ridiculous written down here, and as far as I know no one has ever been sufficiently fooled to try and shoot a midge, but just for the instant it takes to tense your muscles and tighten your grip on your gun a tiny, flying insect can appear, to the mind fully geared to *expect* a grouse to appear at any second, to be that grouse.

Other butts may present the Gun with a clear view for miles in every direction and the chance to watch the beating line grow from tiny dots on the far horizon to discernible figures and finally to recognisable individuals as they plod up to the Guns. These are the type of positions from which you can see grouse moving far out over the heather, rising and falling, perhaps dropping in between beaters and Guns and then getting up again as the beaters come closer. A covey may disappear into a dip in the ground, seemingly miles away, only to appear suddenly right in front of you, rising, swerving and skimming through the line almost before you can mount the gun. Others may be in view for an age keeping you wondering whether they will cross by you or one of your neighbours, trying to work out just how close you need to let them come before mounting the gun, checking your safe arc of fire and feeling your heart thump and your blood pressure rise in anticipation and excitement. After which they may just swerve off to the side and stream over a Gun four places down the line or even slip out of the drive altogether.

Whether you prefer the former type of butt or the latter is largely immaterial in practice since the butts have probably been there for years and years and the luck of the draw will determine where you are placed on each drive. All you have to do is to stand with the gun ready for action, spare cartridges ready to hand in your belt, pocket, cartridge bag or lined up on the rim of the butt according to your choice, and wait for something to happen. If you are lucky enough to be shooting double guns with a loader you might like to have a bit of a rehearsal to make sure that you are both aware of any limitations of space within the butt and how they will affect you when the shooting starts, then you are ready for the grouse to start coming.

So now you are safely ensconced within your butt for the first drive of the day, you have worked out your safe field of fire, perhaps marked it by setting some short sticks in the sides of the butt, had a couple of practice gun mounts, slipped two cartridges into the breech, checked that the safety catch is on, taken a few deep breaths and tried to relax with the scent of heather flowers in your nose and, hopefully, a clear blue sky and a warm August sun overhead. How are you going to shoot your grouse once they start appearing?

I wish that I had such a wealth of experience of driven grouse shooting that I could write several paragraphs of sound advice for the inexperienced grouse Shot based on many years of practice and many thousands of grouse shot. Sadly I do not move in the circles where August and September are crowded with invitations to shoot on all the best moors. Even if I were so favoured there are many different styles and methods of shooting and what works for one Gun may be a recipe for disaster with another. Do you mount and fire in a single movement, pulling the trigger as soon as the gun touches your shoulder, or do you swing smoothly through the bird and ahead, continuing the swing up to and beyond the actual discharge of the gun? Do you watch the birds every yard of the way across the heather and up to the butt, or do you prefer to pick them up only as they come into range and fire instinctively? In practice it doesn't matter how you shoot as long as what you are doing works for you. There is, though, a wealth of information and advice available through books and magazine articles going right back to the days when grouse driving first became fashionable and what I can do is to distil some of that advice down into a brief summary.

All the experts seem to agree on two points. You should, wherever possible, shoot your grouse *in front* of the butt. And you should be selecting your first bird and mounting the gun while they are still well out in front.

To deal with the latter point first, the birds will be coming at you fast and probably low and will close up the gap between themselves and the butts with surprising speed. If you are mounting the gun when they are sixty yards out by the time you have got onto your bird and fired it will be closer to forty yards and it will be flying into the shot. There is a much higher possibility of finding a vulnerable spot and achieving an instant kill than with a bird going away behind the line, increasing the range with every beat of its wings.

If you miss or prick the bird with that first shot you have a little more time for a second shot at it; if you kill it cleanly there is a fraction more time for you to select a second bird and get on to it while they are still out in front. If you shoot your grouse well out there is obviously less chance of spoiling them for the table by peppering them with loads of shot, and there is the additional advantage that the wider your shot pattern has spread the greater your margin of error and thus the greater your chances of actually killing your bird.

Whether you miss both or kill both, if you have fired both barrels in front of the butt you will be facing in the right direction to see if more grouse are coming forward. If you turn and fire behind it is all too easy to miss the next wave of birds altogether if they come through the line while you are turning round to face the front again. And if you are shooting birds well out in front whenever possible the chances of you swinging through the line or turning to take a bird behind without elevating your muzzles to a safe height are greatly reduced. So shoot them in front and shoot them early until the beaters are too close for shooting forwards safely and the horn or the whistle sounds to signal no more shooting in front.

There are times when you will have to turn and take birds behind apart from at the

No shooting forward as the beaters near the butts.

end of each drive when the beaters would be in danger of getting shot. The grouse may be on you and past before you have time to shoot them in front, especially if you are in a butt with limited forward visibility and the birds are screaming through with the wind under their tails. Grouse may not be coming at right-angles to the line of butts and birds that have crossed further along the line may pass behind your butt giving you the chance of a crossing shot. Having got the first shot off in front you may have to turn round if the grouse are too close to the butts for a second shot. And, if you are shooting with double guns you may be able to get two shots in front and then turn, change guns and get two more shots behind thus taking four birds out of each covey. Or three, or two, or one or perhaps none....

Some of the great Shots of old were famous for their ability to take two grouse in front and then two more behind with an easy grace and plenty of time to spare as they changed guns. Some of those old Shots did little else except shoot grouse, day after day from August to the end of September, and probably spent hours practising changing guns with their regular loader who travelled from shoot to shoot with them. You may be in that happy situation yourself even today, and if so I will freely admit to envying you your good fortune.

This Gun has stepped out from the butt at the end of the drive to give himself more freedom to swing onto the grouse.

Shooting with two guns and a loader is almost an art form, requiring no little skill and like most things meeting that description it will improve enormously with practice. Standing in the confines of a grouse butt with birds whistling past your ears is neither the time nor the place to begin learning how to shoot, change guns and shoot again. Barrels are notoriously easy to dent and will not stand up to being dinged against the stone walls of the butt or clattered against the other gun. Two sets of best English barrels coming into contact can result in an extremely expensive repair bill. If you are fortunate enough to be shooting double guns, particularly with a loader you have not shot with previously, then make every effort to get as much practice as possible in before the grouse start arriving and adrenaline and excitement take over.

The theory of changing guns is relatively simple and easily grasped, though it is almost as easily forgotten if the air is full of grouse and you are desperately trying to get four shots off at this covey and then spin round to get more shots away at the next one following closely behind. Assuming that you are right-handed the procedure is as follows.

The loader will be standing behind the Gun, close enough to pass the guns between the two but not so near as to cramp the Gun's ability to swing his gun freely. The Gun fires one or two shots then elevates the muzzles so that they are pointing straight upwards and passes the fired gun back, holding it with his right hand on the stock. The loader grasps the fore end of the fired gun with his left hand while holding the loaded gun with his right hand gripping the stock. At the same time as he is taking the fired gun he places the fore end of the loaded gun into the Gun's left hand, then turns away to eject the spent cartridge(s) and replace them ready to exchange guns again as soon as required.

A loader can be useful in other ways such as spotting grouse that are coming forward to 'his' Gun and keeping a note of how many birds are down and where they fell. However, and this is important, his primary function is to load and to do so quickly and safely without damaging the guns or endangering the other occupants of the butt or of the neighbouring butts. Spotting incoming grouse or marking shot birds should not be allowed to divert attention from the job in hand.

If you are on your own as far as loading goes it is a good idea to ensure that you have cartridges readily available in case you find yourself having to reload in a hurry. Some Guns use the loaders' trick of keeping a couple of cartridges ready between the fingers of their front hand, though on the few occasions that I tried this I found that it just distracted me from my shooting. You can lay out some spare cartridges or place your cartridge bag handily on top of the butt so that you don't have to bend down and lose sight of the moor after every shot. If you are loading from a cartridge belt it may help to have a few cartridges loosened off and standing proud of the rest so that they are easily grasped when you reach for them. Shooting coats often incorporate some means of clipping back the pocket flap to give you instant access if you keep your ammunition in a pocket and there are patent cartridge belts designed to allow you to break out the cartridges from spring clips rather than having them secured in leather loops. Whatever you prefer it is always a good idea to be ready for a quick reload, even if the need never occurs.

What to Wear

There are three major considerations concerning the right clothes for shooting driven grouse. Your clothes obviously have to fulfil the regular shooting clothing requirements of keeping you dry if it is raining and neither allowing you to boil nor freeze depending on the temperature. Then they have to provide you with a degree of camouflage so that the grouse don't spot you from half a mile away and swerve away from your butt, and finally, they need to fall within the fairly wide limits of what is acceptable wear for driven grouse shooting.

The last point is probably the trickiest to define since there are no set rules to guide the novice. Driven grouse shooting has a long history behind it and like many traditional activities, particularly those that date back to Victorian Britain, it is never difficult to make a social gaffe where the 'right' clothing is concerned. Things are further complicated for the beginner because the measure of what is acceptable may vary according to who you are. If 'The Duke' decides to shoot wearing a waxed jacket that has holes in the pockets, is black with mould and held closed with string because the zip is broken he will be considered charmingly eccentric where I would be classed as a scruffy oik who ought to have made some effort to at least try to look respectable. On some shoots a brand new tweed suit with matching hat would draw looks bearing just a trace of contempt from more experienced guns dressed in hand-me-down tweeds that would be turned away by a charity shop.

It is a fact that on many grouse moors on the Twelfth of August the keeper will present a far smarter appearance than the man who is paying his wages. The keeper will have put on his best tweed suit for the occasion, and there is a good possibility that it will be brand new as most keepers' contracts of employment provide for a new suit every season. The moor owner may well be wearing a tweed suit that belonged to his father. The difference is that the keeper will wear his suit practically every day of the year and quickly wear it out whereas even the owner of a grouse moor may only shoot a dozen times each season so that it would take thirty years for his suit to get the same amount of wear as that of the keeper.

Looking the part, whether for grouse shooting or any other activity, is something that seems to come naturally and easily to some people while being permanently beyond the reach of others – even if they are dressed in identical outfits. Perhaps the best advice for someone who is going grouse shooting for the first time is to look at some shooting magazines to see what other people are wearing and to avoid extremes. A collar and tie always looks better than an open necked shirt, and boots or shoes should start the day in a clean and polished state. I suppose the most important thing is that you feel comfortable with what you are wearing in the mental as well as the physical sense.

And it is your physical comfort that we will consider next. As we have seen already grouse moors are subject to extremes of weather from baking heat to bitter cold, from blazing sunshine to driving rain, and unless you are in the middle of a really settled spell of weather you will need to be prepared for any or all of the above.

Obviously you should pay attention to the weather forecast and to the look of the sky on the day of the shoot when deciding what to wear. The driven grouse Shot is at a considerable advantage over the man who is walking the moor in pursuit of his sport because he can shed layers of clothing in the butt whereas the walking gun who removes his coat will still have it to carry. To a considerable extent your choice of clothing will be influenced by the way that shooting is organised on the moor you are visiting.

If the Guns are conveyed between drives by some form of vehicle, and if the butts are always conveniently situated within a few yards of the hill roads then a pair of brogues might be ideal wear for the feet. If though you are going to have to walk from drive to drive through the heather and perhaps climb a thousand feet up the hill to

A big covey sweeping through the butts with one grouse shot in front…

…and a second one killed behind.

reach the topmost butt in the line you would be better served by a good pair of walking boots and a set of gaiters. A sunken butt with a well-drained gravel floor would be fine for the man wearing the brogues, but if heavy rain had left three inches of water accumulated in the butt he might soon be wishing he had worn a pair of wellies instead. If you don't know what to expect and have no means of finding out then it is always better to be prepared to dress for the more extreme situation. If you are travelling in your own vehicle then you can take along a selection of kit and decide what is appropriate when you have spoken to your host, the keeper and the other Guns, but if you are uncertain about conditions and have to make a choice of clothing in advance then I would suggest that you err on the side of caution. Wearing walking boots when brogues would have been sufficient simply means you are slightly over-shod; wearing brogues when you really need walking boots or wellies may mean an unpleasant day with soaking wet feet.

By the same token, if you are going to have access to a vehicle between drives you can bring along extra clothes – waterproof coat and leggings, pullover, gloves, etc. – and add or shed layers as the day gets warmer and drier or perhaps colder and wetter. Even if you are walking from drive to drive it is easy enough to shed as many layers as required for comfort once you are installed in your butt, and if you have an obliging loader you may even be able to persuade him to carry all your extra gear for you. And if he does, I trust you will remember this act of kindness when it comes to handing over a tip at the end of the shoot.

Whatever you are wearing, it needs to be free-fitting enough to allow you to swing the gun quickly and easily. The chance of a shot can come and go very swiftly and a coat that drags across the shoulders or is tight under the arms may just be enough to make the difference between failure and success. You may get away with it shooting pheasants when you can see the birds coming from a long way out and mount the gun deliberately, but when it comes to whipping the gun up to the shoulder and snapping off a quick shot at a grouse that suddenly bursts into view forty yards ahead any restriction of movement can be fatal – though not for the grouse.

The question of camouflage or concealment is almost as important as keeping warm/cool and dry. Some Shots would argue that it is even more important, since a cold wet gun can still shoot if the grouse come over his butt whereas no matter how comfortable and at ease you are, if the grouse swerve away from your position in the line inevitably your shooting will be curtailed.

It is not necessary to go to the lengths that a woodland deer-stalker might adopt with camouflaged coat, trousers, boots, socks, gloves, hat, scarf and face mask. Indeed, if you are sufficiently keen on camouflage patterns to purchase them you can also get camouflaged Thermos flasks, rifle slips, binoculars, telescopes and even underwear. I cannot envisage a situation where anyone would be close enough to a deer to need camouflaged Y-fronts, but you may have a more vivid imagination than me. I merely point out that they are available if you feel the need.

But there is no need to dress from head to toe in some exotic shell-suit that supposedly resembles trees and leaves, or brush and grass, or whatever type of background the pattern is supposed to represent. All that is required is that your shooting outfit is made of some suitably muted cloth that will not stand out against the moorland background. Almost any pattern of tweed will do – in fact any coat or jacket designed for shooting will almost certainly be made in colours that are chosen so as to be unobtrusive – and unobtrusive is what you require. The chances are that you will be concealed in a butt from at least the waist and possibly from the shoulders down, so the important bits are the chest and head.

I am not suggesting that you should wear a tweed jacket over Day-Glo orange trousers, but in practice, as long as the jacket was tastefully bland in colour you would probably not be handicapped as far as the grouse were concerned. What your host and the rest of the participants might think and/or say about it is another matter. What you should avoid is wearing anything very light or bright where it will be visible to the grouse. Incidentally, black is not a good colour for the moors either and very dark clothes can be almost as visible as very light ones in some circumstances. In general though if you stick to clothes that are quiet and muted when seen at a distance you shouldn't have problems with grouse spotting you and swerving away from your butt.

Changing guns with eyes looking firmly ahead ready for the next covey.

I use the phrase 'at a distance' because some of the shooting tweeds can be quite lurid when seen close up but will still blend into the background when seen from further away. A hat or cap is important too because a white face will stand out from a long way away no matter how well concealed the rest of the body may be. If you have a full head of hair and a deep sun tan or perhaps a full beard you may get away without wearing a hat but it is best to err on the side of caution and wear one anyway. A peak of some sort can be useful in keeping the sun out of your eyes or the rain off your glasses and may even lend a degree of protection if someone fires a careless shot from further along the line.

On a cold day gloves may be useful provided that they don't stop you from loading quickly after taking a shot, though most grouse are shot before the really cold weather sets in. If you like to err on the side of caution, or if you know your fellow guns may be a little excitable, a pair of safety glasses could be a good investment. Most guns these days seem to wear ear defenders and it certainly makes sense to protect your hearing since gun deafness is still incurable as far as I am aware.

Other Equipment

There is not a great deal that you really need for driven grouse shooting other than suitable clothing, a gun and some cartridges, but there are few things that you might find useful. There can often be quite a long wait before the action starts because of the vast acreages that are brought in and a shooting stick will provide you with a reasonably comfortable seat while allowing you to keep an eye on the moor and be more or less ready to shoot if a bird sneaks through unexpectedly. If you have a retriever with you and it is anything less than one hundred per cent reliable as far as running in is concerned you should have some means of securing it within the butt until the end of the drive. With grouse flying low to the ground and the contour of the moor often meaning that butts are built at differing heights, a dog that is running about in front or behind the line during the drive has a very reasonable chance of being shot accidentally.

A lead and something to fasten it to are advisable unless you are absolutely certain your dog will not run in – and it is not a bad idea even then. A stick driven well into the peat, one of those patent corkscrew things or your companion in the butt if you happen to have one can be used to keep the dog safe until the drive is over. Do not be tempted to use your cartridge bag or your gun slip or anything else that a determined dog can drag along behind itself, and under no circumstance loop the lead around your shooting stick. I write from painful experience in this having once been unceremoniously dumped on the ground by a normally placid Labrador who couldn't wait to collect a pheasant that my neighbour had just shot.

Cameras and binoculars can provide a diversion, but beware of letting them become too much of a diversion – it is all too easy to be busy taking pictures of your neighbour just when a covey swings over your own position. A gamebag is not usually needed but it can be useful for carrying a flask, spare boxes of cartridges, a lightweight set of waterproofs and anything else you might feel will be useful during or between drives. If you do collect any shot game it will also be handy for carrying it back to the game cart or whatever is being used as a collecting point for the shot birds.

You will need something to keep cartridges ready to hand for reloading. This can be a cartridge bag, a cartridge belt or simply your coat pocket. If you are shooting with double guns this will be the responsibility of your loader. Whatever you are using have a practice run before the action starts to ensure that you can get cartridges quickly and easily while within the confines of the butt. Some butts are quite a tight fit and it is easy to ding the barrels against the sides when you are grabbing for spare ammunition, and generally butts are built of fairly unforgiving materials as far as gun barrels are concerned. You can keep a supply in a pocket and replace them from your belt or bag as they are depleted, or you can lay a few spares on the wall of the butt for the moments when the grouse are coming thick and fast.

Guns for Driven Grouse

As already noted, for most people the gun they use for driven grouse will be the gun they use for everything else they shoot. That said, lots of us have more than one gun, many guns are fitted with adjustable choke systems of one kind or another and a lucky few may be planning to buy a new gun especially for driven grouse shooting so a few thoughts on gun choice may be useful.

When grouse are pouring through the butts care must be taken not to swing through the line.

In general the problems presented by driven grouse are not concerned with shooting birds at very long ranges. There may be drives where the butts are placed low down in a gully, or where the butts are so far apart that high or long shots will be presented, but most of the time grouse tend to fly quite close to the ground and butts are usually set at quite close spacings. When shot in front of the butt the grouse will be closing the range quite swiftly and where butts are placed with limited forward visibility ranges may be quite short by the time the birds have been spotted and the gun mounted.

The grouse is not a difficult bird to kill being soft feathered and quite a bit smaller than a pheasant. There is no need for large sizes of shot nor excessively high velocity cartridges. Where birds are closing in on the Gun and may in any case have to be shot at relatively close range the most successful combination is likely to be a gun that throws a wide spread of shot with a decent pattern so that you will not be missing or wounding birds because there is not a sufficient density of shot. It might seem logical to conclude that the ideal gun for driven grouse would be bored something like improved cylinder in both barrels and fire an ounce and a bit of number six shot. And such a combination would probably be an excellent grouse gun if we assume that it was a twelve bore and thus suitable for throwing an ounce and an eighth or an ounce and a quarter of shot.

However, the popularity of smaller, lighter guns such as sixteen, twenty and twenty-eight bores means that we must look a little closer at the matters of choke and load. In my opinion – which you are at liberty to disregard – there is little sense in trying to put twelve bore loads through a twenty bore gun. You can buy twenty bore cartridges loaded with an ounce and more of shot but if you want to use that amount of shot a twelve bore will handle it better. A small bore gun firing a large load will either kick unacceptably or have to be built to the same weight as a larger gun. If your twenty bore weighs the same as a twelve bore then you might as well have the twelve bore, which will probably throw a better pattern anyway because of the length of the shot column. So let us assume that, if you are using a small bore gun you will be firing small bore loads from it.

That being the case you may require a greater degree of choke in your barrels in order to ensure that the pattern is sufficiently dense to be effective against a bird the size of a grouse. You can overcome this to some extent by dropping a shot size, but I would suggest that anything less than size seven is likely to lack the striking energy needed to ensure a quick, clean kill. Therefore, as you drop down in size from the ubiquitous twelve bore you should probably also consider a slight increase in the amount of choke in order to compensate for the decreased shot load.

There is though the matter of shooting behind to consider. Where grouse shot in front of the butt will normally be flying into your shot pattern and decreasing the distance from you with some speed, the opposite is true of grouse shot behind the butt. They will be departing with considerable enthusiasm, spurred on by the sound of shots and the sight of men and they will also be a little less vulnerable than when they are coming towards you with their heads and necks exposed. A case can now be made

The best place to shoot driven grouse is out in front of the butt.

for tight chokes to maximise the range at which the birds can be taken as they fly away from you and heavier shot to increase the striking energy.

Obviously you have to compromise between the open-bored gun that is suited to oncoming birds and the rather more tightly choked barrels that may be required when the grouse are disappearing swiftly behind the butt. Personally I would err on the more open side since the aim in most cases is to take the birds out in front as far as possible. Even so, at the end of each drive there is likely to be a brief period when shooting in front is forbidden, and on some drives this may be the most productive part. The choice is yours, in so far as you have a choice and are not restricted to shooting with your regular game gun.

As far as weight and barrel length are concerned it is simply a matter of shooting with the gun that suits your style of shooting. There is a case to be made for the grouse gun to be light-weight and fitted with short barrels to increase the speed at which it can be mounted, pointed and swung, and in theory a gun built with twenty-five inch barrels ought to be ideal. In practice some Guns shoot abominably with short barrels finding that they seem to wave around almost at random. If your style of shooting is best served by long barrels and the extra inertia they lend to your swing there is no point in investing in a short-barrelled weapon. You will kill more grouse with the gun that suits you than with a gun designed to suit grouse.

Grouse Keepering

The moorland keeper differs from most of his low ground counterparts in that he is concerned solely with wild birds. Pheasants, partridges and ducks can all be reared and released allowing a shoot to be as productive, within reason, as time and money will allow. A few hundred birds to boost the wild stock or tens of thousands to allow a shoot to be run on a commercial basis: the amount of shooting available within any one season is pretty much within the control of the shoot management. On a grouse moor the numbers are reliant on the vagaries of the weather, predation, disease and various other factors largely outside the control of the owner and the keepering staff.

This is not to suggest that all the owner of a grouse moor need do is turn up on the Twelfth of August and see how many birds have survived and multiplied since the last day of the previous season. Left entirely to nature most moorland will quickly degenerate into scrub woodland if it lies below the tree line. The heather will grow long and rank, predation will reduce the stock of grouse to subsistence levels and shooting may no longer be a viable option. Certainly, on some moors a stock of grouse would survive any amount of neglect. The grouse existed in considerable numbers before hunting them for sport first encouraged man to try and manage their environment, and in many parts of the world members of the grouse family survive today in a completely wild state with no interference from man at all. But the familiar 'wild' landscape of the British grouse moor is largely one that has been created by man and without his continued interference much of the moorland as we know it would disappear.

Over the past three centuries man has discovered, partly by accident but mainly by design, the best ways to manage heather moorland in order to encourage the red grouse to thrive naturally – though perhaps 'naturally' should be in inverted commas in this case. Attempts have been made to rear grouse in the same way that pheasants and partridges are produced for release but so far no one has found a way to do this in quantity. Grouse eggs can be gathered and hatched in incubators and under broody hens and the chicks can be reared to maturity, but not in sufficient numbers to make it a viable alternative to traditional keepering work. It may be that some day a way will be found to produce grouse by the thousand and to release them successfully onto heather moorland and no doubt there would be enormous commercial benefits from such an enterprise. Whether it would benefit the red grouse or the sport of grouse shooting are other matters and open to debate.

Grouse keepering is primarily concerned with two elements: improving the environment and reducing predation. There are of course many other things to occupy the grouse keeper: building and repairing butts, maintaining roads and tracks, organising shooting days, dealing with the general public, guarding against poachers, training dogs and looking after the vehicles and equipment necessary for his work. He may also be involved in low ground shooting, perhaps having pheasants and partridges to look after as well as grouse and the keeper often doubles up as the shepherd responsible for any sheep on the moor. If there are deer on the ground he may have to carry out an annual cull, perhaps guiding stalking guests as well. A river, lochs or lakes may mean trout and salmon fishing lie within his area of work so he may be a ghillie during the fishing season as well as a stalker and a keeper and a shepherd. A grouse keeper is rarely short of work even though he has no rearing field or release pens to occupy his time.

Heather Burning

The great explosion in the population of grouse during the nineteenth century came about largely because it was discovered that regular burning of the heather provided the grouse with the fresh, young shoots that are their preferred diet. Old heather becomes woody, rank and less nutritious: burning it allows new growth to take place from the old rootstock and grouse thrive on this new growth and the better the food supply the better most animals and birds will thrive. At the same time though, the grouse must have somewhere to hide from predators, to shelter from the weather and to conceal their nests. Long heather fulfils all of these functions so a grouse moor must consist of part long heather for cover and part short heather for food. The job of the keeper is to burn the heather during the winter and spring months in order to create this desirable environment.

Given dry weather – and that condition may be difficult to impossible to achieve in some years – it is quite simple to burn heather. All you need is a box of matches and a bit of a breeze and one man could burn a whole moor in a day, though there might be problems stopping the fire at the day's end. Unfortunately proper heather burning requires a degree more care than that which translates into an awful lot of hard, hot work for the keeper and any assistants that he may be able to call upon. Since heather burning is so dependent on weather conditions being right – dry, with not too strong a wind – during precisely those months when such conditions are least likely to occur,

A tractor fitted with a swipe for cutting firebreaks through the heather.

it is impossible to plan far in advance. In an ideal world the keeper would block in so many weeks in his diary for burning heather, engage suitable labour for the job and have the whole thing wrapped up on time and on budget. In practice burning has to take place as and when it is possible with a day snatched here and there whenever conditions allow.

It is rarely practical to have enough men on standby ready to come to the moor at a moment's notice. In the old days, when labour was cheap and readily available and money was in plentiful supply some moor owners did just that, paying a gang of men a retainer on condition that they would be on hand whenever conditions allowed the heather to be burnt. Today there can be few if any moor owners who would contemplate that sort of expense and indeed with modern methods of burning there are better ways to spend the money on such things as tractors and swipes, of which more later.

The ideal habitat for the red grouse would consist of short, fresh heather for food with longer heather close by for shelter. One large fire that spreads over many acres is of far less benefit than a series of small fires covering the same total acreage but spread out across the moor with patches of longer heather in between. This is easily planned in principle using a pencil and a map of the moor and – in principle – should result in a perfect geometric pattern of long and short strips of heather alternating from boundary to boundary. In practice conditions on the ground tend to have some effect on how close to the ideal is the actuality.

The ideal pattern for burning heather is to have a patchwork quilt effect of strips of heather of differing lengths. Heather will grow at differing rates depending on how far north the moor is situated, the height above sea level, the weather and the mineral content of the ground beneath its roots. Where conditions are ideal it might be feasible to burn the heather on a ten year rotation: i.e. burn one tenth of the moor each year, starting back at the beginning in the eleventh year by which time the first areas burnt should be ready for firing again. Other moors might need closer to twenty years for the heather to grow to the same degree and obviously the plan for burning needs to take this into account.

There is also the problem that in some years the weather may dictate that there will be little or no burning done at all. Other years may have long spells of ideal weather at just the right time. In practice the keeper will have to make the most of the proper conditions whenever they occur so some years may see more heather burnt than would be indicated by a simple, regular rotation. Provided that some degree of moderation is exercised it is unlikely that too much heather will be burnt and it is practically certain that within the next year or two wet and windy weather will bring things back to plan.

Burning the moor in strips means controlling the limits of each fire after it has been kindled. Sometimes this can be done by using naturally occurring fire-breaks such as rivers, streams, lochs, scree slopes, roadways, bogs and peat hags, but most of the time the fires must be controlled manually. The traditional way of doing this was to use birch brooms to beat out the edges of the fires.

In shortish heather with a gentle breeze it can be quite an easy task to stroll along beside the fire and pat out the odd tongue of flame that tries to creep

Cutting breaks through dry heather.

away from the area that you want to be burnt. Just one or two men can light, control and extinguish the strips of heather and control the flames with ease. When the breeze has risen and the heather is long and dry it can be a choking, sweating, skin-scorching nightmare of smoke and flames as you desperately try to prevent the fire raging across the whole moor or leaping into a couple of thousand acres of valuable timber just over the march. Mostly the work falls somewhere in between those extremes: hard and hot but not actually life-threatening and, on a good day, a tiring but very satisfying job with something to show for all the hard work at the end of the day.

Birch brooms are still used along with various other types of beater made of wire mesh, rubber belting or old shovel blades. As long as the head of the broom can be used to beat out and smother the flames it will be effective. A long handle is essential since the burning heather generates a great deal of heat and smoke and the further back you can stand while still being able to reach the flames the better you will be able to control them. Protective clothing is advisable: gloves and a face mask will allow you to get a little closer to the heat without losing your eyebrows and the hair on the back of your hands. The rest of your clothes should be thick enough to protect you from the heat and old enough so that you won't mind them getting scorched and stinking of smoke. Especially avoid synthetic fibres like nylon that have a tendency to melt when exposed to extremes of heat. If you wear Wellington boots it is as well to have your trousers outside the boots so that a burning brand of heather won't drop down inside them.

Heather can be burnt in two ways: up wind and down wind. Burning with the wind behind the fire gives a less intense burn as the flames roll across the heather quite quickly and leave long burnt stalks sticking out of the ashes. Burning into the wind means that the fire will be hotter and travel much more slowly as it creeps through the heather and leaves clean, bare ground behind it. There are differing opinions as to which is the most effective method and to some extent conditions on the ground will dictate which can be used. If for example the wind is blowing towards a forestry block it makes sense to burn into the wind and away from danger.

Up-wind burning requires that the fire is initially prevented from setting off in the natural direction – i.e. down wind – as soon as the heather is lighted. This can be done by setting fires where there is some sort of natural firebreak – a road, stream, wet area or the site of a previous burn – or by controlling the flames with beaters until there is a sufficient area of burnt ground to prevent it creeping back into the un-burnt heather. This can be extremely hot work since in order to control the fire the beaters will have to work right in among the smoke and the heat from the flames, but once in control up-wind fires generally burn away steadily and are relatively easy to control compared to the inferno that can occur when a fire gets a good grip among long heather with a fresh breeze to whip it along.

Ideally a keeper planning to control fires in the traditional way would have plenty of extra labourers on hand. When things are going well they can be split up into gangs of two or three, lighting and controlling fires across the area to be burnt. If a fire gets out

The swipe in cutting position…

…and showing the chains that whirl round to cut the heather.

143

of hand they can quickly be concentrated where most needed in order to restore control as soon as possible. In practice there will often be only one gang of two or three men available and if a fire does run wild they may be in considerable trouble unless they can get help and get it fairly urgently. If they are lucky there may be shepherds or neighbouring keepers who can come to their aid though given the nature of grouse moors it is likely to be quite some time before they will arrive. In the last resort the local fire brigade may be called out though even they may be helpless when confronted with a really major fire that has had time to take a good hold across a wide front.

The modern approach to heather burning relies less on labour and more on machinery. A tractor fitted with a swipe can cut firebreaks quickly and easily, provided that there is access to the moor and that the ground is flat enough and firm enough to take heavy machinery. The principle is simple. The tractor driver cuts a firebreak around each strip to be burnt and the heather within the firebreak is ignited by the man with

Lighting a line of heather using a plumber's torch.

The fire soon gets under way.

Working hard with a broom to control the spread of the flames.

the matches. Once it is burning satisfactorily he moves on to the next strip, and the next. If everything is going absolutely to plan each fire will burn itself out when it reaches the cut heather and the moor will be left with a geometrically perfect pattern of long and short heather.

In practice it is essential to keep an eye on the fires to make sure that they don't jump or creep across the firebreaks. A slight incursion can usually be controlled by a man with a beater, and if a fire does get away it should be relatively easy to stop by cutting a break with the swipe in its line of march. Moors that have been burnt using a mechanical swipe are easily recognised because of the straight edges to most of the burnt patches.

It might seem that it would be feasible to simply cut the heather with the swipe and not bother burning at all. While this would certainly result in a mixture of long and short heather in practice it is much less beneficial to the moor and the grouse than burning the heather. Cut heather can form a blanket over the ground that turns wet and mouldy and smothers the new growth. More importantly, burning actually helps the heather to regenerate and burnt ground will produce better young heather than ground that has been swiped. The smoke from burning stimulates the heather seeds and improves germination; indeed; there are experiments ongoing as I write into finding the best way to treat heather seed with smoke prior to re-seeding moors where the heather has been taken over by rough grass and rushes.

There is a limited market for cut heather to be used in filter beds to prevent the smell from industrial processes such as rendering plants polluting the air. While this could only be of interest to a very limited number of moors it is possible that for some owners it might provide an additional source of income and perhaps help with heather burning by creating firebreaks through the longest heather.

Predator Control

There is no benefit in creating the ideal habitat for grouse if all the birds simply disappear down the throats of predators. Controlling the various animals and birds that prey on grouse, grouse eggs and grouse chicks is a vital part of every moorland keeper's work. It is also the most controversial area of that work and one that has the potential to bring him into conflict with various interest groups and with the law.

It is well established that the number of predators is directly linked to the abundance of prey. When voles are abundant barn owls thrive, when voles are scarce they decline. In a good vole year the owls may raise three or four young; in a bad year one or none. The same applies to practically all predators. When prey is abundant they thrive and multiply; when prey is scarce they starve and decline. In the case of a grouse moor Man has added himself to the list of species that prey on the red grouse and, given that he is investing a great deal of time and money, he hopes to take the major part of any surplus that is available. Unfortunately the local foxes, crows, stoats, mink, badgers, hedgehogs, hen harriers, buzzards, peregrine falcons and goshawks do not subscribe to this ideal.

A few years ago the Langholm Experiment was jointly run by the Game and Wildlife Conservation Trust and the Royal Society for the Protection of Birds (RSPB). The Langolm moors were a productive part of the Buccleuch Estates and were made available by the Duke of Buccleuch for research into hen harriers and their effect on the red grouse. Over around five years the keepers continued to control foxes and crows, to burn the heather and provide grit for the grouse while the hen harriers were allowed to flourish and hunt the moor under the watchful eye of the RSPB. The results were interesting to say the least.

By the end of five years the harriers had multiplied to the extent that there were very few grouse left for them to hunt. The moor was effectively finished as far as grouse shooting was concerned since there were no longer enough grouse to make shooting viable. Keepering ceased and the keepers were redeployed elsewhere. A moor that had made a valuable contribution to the local economy ceased to provide employment or to attract sportsmen to the area. Ironically, with no control of foxes and crows being carried out and with only limited food supplies the hen harrier population quickly declined back to the point at which it had begun. The RSPB, who had hoped to establish that grouse and hen harriers could live in peace and harmony, were embarrassed by the obvious conclusions to be drawn from the experiment: that unless there is a measure of control on birds of prey grouse shooting is not viable.

Part of the problem appeared to be that with the foxes and crows that would take harrier eggs and chicks being controlled there were no factors to limit the growth in harrier numbers until they exceeded the capacity of the moor to support them. Once the keepers were no longer killing crows and foxes the harriers themselves were subject to predation at the same time as their food supply was running out and their decline was swift though not, sadly, accompanied by a resurgence in grouse numbers.

But the implications of the experiment go further than the survival or otherwise of hen harriers. Grouse shooting is of enormous economic benefit to large areas of England and Scotland that would otherwise offer little or no employment prospects to the local population. Moorland management creates and maintains a unique and valuable habitat for many species of birds, insects and animals besides the red grouse and in particular provides protection for ground nesting birds such as skylarks, curlews, oyster catchers, peewits and golden plovers that struggle to survive where predation and modern farming practices threaten their eggs, nests and chicks. If grouse shooting becomes unviable then keepering ceases, predation increases and other forms of moorland management such as forestry or sheep farming take over. And all too quickly, the grouse, the heather moorland and the birds and animals that lived on it are lost to be replaced by serried ranks of foreign softwoods or bracken, rushes and rough grass.

Ultimately, a blind insistence on the protection of all birds of prey no matter what the consequences threatens the existence of the very creatures that are supposedly being protected. Take away the control of foxes, crows, stoats and mink, allow the heather to be replaced with trees or rough grazing, let the grouse, the curlew, the lark and the pipit suffer predation and loss of habitat and the predators will soon outstrip

Other moorland birds such as these lapwings benefit from the work of the keeper.

the available food supply with predictable consequences. Take away the keeper, stop burning the heather, let the grouse decline to the point at which shooting becomes uneconomic and the surplus of prey that allowed the predators to multiply will quickly disappear. If there is not enough food to sustain them the predator population will decline just as surely as will that of the prey. When the heather is gone, the keeper has been made redundant, the grouse are gone and the harriers have been starved out of existence it is difficult to see who has benefited.

Yet so blinkered are the pressure groups that they refuse to listen to men who have spent all their lives working on the hill and the moor, nor will they accept the scientific evidence gleaned from their own researches. They also seem to have an undue level of influence with the police in many areas. In my part of Scotland if someone steals money from you by fraudulent misuse of your credit card the police will not even investigate the crime, but when the RSPB made an allegation that a local keeper had poisoned a buzzard they were able to spare fifty officers – yes, fifty – to conduct a dawn raid on the estate where he worked. And that was by no means an unusual response to unsubstantiated accusations of this nature.

Whatever your feelings on the matter the fact remains that all raptors: kites, buzzards, hawks, falcons, owls, eagles, ospreys and harriers: are protected by the law and any keeper harming, or attempting to harm any bird of that ilk will be prosecuted if he is caught. And be under no illusions; the police and the various wildlife organisations devote a great deal of time and effort to try and catch any keeper who elects to break the law. The penalties are severe: heavy fines, the loss of firearms and shotgun certificates and quite possibly a prison sentence await any keeper found guilty of 'wildlife crime'. In addition his job and home may also be forfeit since, whatever he might think privately, it would be difficult for a landowner to keep in his employ a keeper with a conviction for killing a bird of prey.

The low ground keeper has a readily available solution to offset the losses caused by predation by protected species. Where pheasants or partridges are reared and released it is simple enough to increase stocking rates so as to cancel out the numbers killed by predators. It may be an expensive option, but it is a simple and legal way of countering the loss of birds to predators. Unfortunately such a solution is not available to the grouse moor keeper. Predation, if left unchecked, can threaten not only his own livelihood and that of other local workers and businesses but, ultimately, the existence of the very habitat and associated wildlife that the law is supposed to protect. There is an almost unanswerable case for giving special status to moorland keepers and allowing them to control raptors within properly agreed and defined limits. I find it difficult to see such a sensible move ever being allowed though.

In reality the only advice that can possibly be offered to grouse keepers is that they must stay within the law. Whether the law will ever be amended so as to enable the moorland keeper to control predators in a way that will benefit not only the grouse but also all the other ground-nesting birds found in this unique environment is doubtful. Powerful pressure groups and weak governments are a bad combination. Why organisations with no economic interest and often with no real grip on reality should be allowed to dictate to the landowners and gamekeepers who rely on the land for their livelihood beggars belief – but that is Britain in the twenty-first century.

Having got that out of the way let us return to the predator control that moorland keepers can and do carry out. There are three main targets for the keeper: the fox, the crow family and the stoat, plus a number of minor offenders such as mink, feral cats, rats, weasels, and feral ferrets. The degree to which some of these may be a problem will depend to a considerable extent on where the moor is situated. If you are surrounded by forestry then foxes and crows are likely to be much more of a problem than if your ground is completely ringed about by other, keepered grouse moors. Low ground and woodlands offer cover for fox earths and trees for nesting crows that can raid over the boundaries. Modern forestry management methods make the keeper's job even more difficult since the woods are often virtually impenetrable and offer foxes and crows safe havens where they can breed with impunity.

The moorland keeper does not have the pheasant or partridge keeper's options of protecting his birds from predation by the use of release pens and electric fences. The

Well built butt made of stone and topped off with turfs of heather.

Building and maintaining butts is an important part of the grouse keeper's duties.

grouse have only their own inherited instincts to guide them in choosing nest sites and keeping their chicks from predators. The keeper's aim is to minimise the number of those predators by such means as are legally available to him. These have been considerably restricted over the last century, often with good cause. Devices such as the pole trap were banned in the early years of the twentieth century and with good reason. Although undoubtedly effective against hawks, falcons and owls and especially so on grouse moors where places for a predator to perch are limited, the pole trap was a barbaric device that left its victims dangling by their broken legs for hours or even days at a time. We are well rid of it.

Poison was once the moorland keeper's mainstay against crows and foxes. Eggs injected with poison were laid all over the moor in spring and accounted for numerous crows and foxes. They also accounted for anything else that ate them including badgers, hedgehogs, dogs and even, on rare occasions, an unfortunate human. Similarly rabbit carcasses were treated with various concoctions and left for scavengers to find and fresh kills by hawks and falcons were treated with a pinch of poison and left where they lay in case the predator returned to the victim.

The advantage of poisons from the keeper's point of view was that they worked for twenty-four hours a day. The disadvantage was that they were completely indiscriminate in their choice of victim and the baited rabbit set for crows or foxes would just as surely kill buzzards, eagles, cats or dogs if they were the ones to find and eat it. Some poisons such as strychnine would not only kill the bird or animal that took the poisoned bait but would also kill anything that ate the victim.

Effectively *all* use of poison to control predators is illegal today with the exception of baits laid for rats and mice and under certain conditions, grey squirrels. That some keepers – a very small minority – do still use poisons cannot be denied since every year a few cases of poisoning of raptors reach the courts and the newspapers. Such incidents do the shooting world no favours since they help to reinforce the views of those opposed to fieldsports and provide ammunition for those pressure groups and political parties who seek to ban shooting as well as hunting. Severe fines and even prison sentences await any keeper convicted of poisoning birds of prey and quite possibly the loss of his job and home as well. Increasing access to the countryside by the public means that the chances of anyone setting poisoned baits being caught is much greater now than in the past and, incidentally, means that the chances of a pet dog or even a child becoming a victim are greatly increased. Whatever the temptation, keepers should restrict their use of poison to the rats and mice and concentrate on other, legal methods of predator control.

The most used legal methods of controlling predators are shooting and trapping. The most important time for predator control is in the spring months when the grouse are nesting and raising their young, though there is no time of the year when any chance to reduce the predator population should be passed up. In the spring though, killing a fox, a crow or a stoat before it has the chance to raise a family can remove the need to kill a whole bunch of them later in the year. And it is at nesting time and during the first few weeks after hatching that grouse and their young are most vulnerable to predation.

Both the shotgun and the rifle are important in the control of predators. The keeper who carries a gun over his arm whenever practical will at least have the chance of adding the odd crow, stoat, mink or fox to his tally of predators whenever a target of opportunity arises. Certainly if you don't have the gun with you there is no chance whatsoever of accounting for the crows that float tantalisingly just above your head. It sometimes seems as though crows in particular can distinguish between an armed and an unarmed man. As far as predator control on the moor goes though the rifle is probably the more important weapon.

Lamping foxes is a comparatively recent method of controlling the major mammalian predator of the grouse moors – recent in this case referring to the last forty/fifty years or so. In part at least this is because the building of hill roads and the increased availability of off-road vehicles have made it possible for keepers to lamp over much greater areas of moorland than would have been the case in the immediate post-war years. Also, where the early lampers used an old car headlight wired to a heavy battery the modern keeper has a wide range of easily portable spotlights to choose from with narrow beams specifically designed for hunting foxes.

The principles of lamping are simple. The keeper goes out at night armed with a rifle and a powerful spotlight. Foxes – and any other creatures that are abroad – can be spotted by the reflection of their eyes in the beam of the lamp. If the fox is in rifle range it can be shot; if it is too far out it may be possible to lure it closer by 'squeaking' it in. And that, very briefly, sums up lamping foxes.

It is somewhat strange that a fox, caught in the beam of a million candlepower lamp will often carry on about its nocturnal business with little or no regard for the fact that it is lit up like an actor on the stage and will even trot in along the beam in response to a squeak that may – just possibly – sound like a rabbit in distress. Nevertheless, thousands of foxes are killed each year by lamping and for some people it has become a sport in its own right with permission to lamp being eagerly sought by enthusiasts with no ground of their own. While having volunteer labour eager and willing to assist in the control of foxes might seem to be of great benefit to a busy keeper there are negative as well as positive aspects to the surge in the popularity of lamping.

A centre-fire rifle, even in the smaller calibres such as .222 or 22/250 can kill at a very long distances. It is essential that anyone using a rifle at night has an intimate knowledge of the ground to ensure that a missed shot, or a bullet that passes right through a fox, does not go on to kill a sheep or a cow or even an unsuspecting person far away from the intended victim. It may seem like a statement of the obvious, but it is also essential that a shot is only taken when it is absolutely certain that the eyes in the spotlight belong to a fox and not some other animal that is abroad during the hours of darkness. The eyes of badgers, sheep, deer, dogs and humans are easily mistaken for those of a fox and a hasty or thoughtless shot can have fatal consequences for the unintended victim.

The fact that animals such as foxes and deer are conditioned to the sight and sound

One stone butt in the gully and an elevated wooden butt to give the next Gun a bit more forward vision.

of motor vehicles and generally ignore them where the presence of a man on foot would cause immediate flight is a vital factor in the growth of lamping as a means of fox control. It is also a considerable problem for many keepers since it means that deer poachers operating from a vehicle can be on the ground, kill their victims, load them up and be away again long before the keeper or the police can hope to catch them. Modern and even more sophisticated equipment such as night-vision rifle-scopes and binoculars have made detection of such criminals even more difficult for the keeper. A powerful spotlight criss-crossing the moor is visible for miles, but the combination of night-vision equipment and a silenced rifle make detecting and apprehending poachers extremely difficult.

That said, lamping and the legitimate use of night-vision equipment has given the moorland keeper a considerable advantage in his attempts to keep the fox population under control and looks likely to remain the major means of controlling foxes for the foreseeable future.

Bridge trap for small ground predators set above a rocky burn.

Trapping is the other major weapon in the keeper's armoury. Again, where once virtually any type of trap could be set at will there are now laws prescribing what type of trap may be set for various predators and the conditions under which they must be managed. Broadly, there are several types of live capture traps, spring traps and snares.

The snare is principally used against the fox, though where rabbits are a problem snaring is a common means of controlling their numbers. The law requires that all snares are free-running – that is to say that the old design of self-locking snare is now illegal – and are inspected at least once per day. It is also advisable to incorporate a stop to prevent sheep, deer or cattle being caught by their legs.

Spring traps are mostly used to control small ground predators such as stoats, rats and weasels and are designed to kill their victims quickly by catching them around the body rather than by the legs as did the old gin-trap. They must not be set in the open where birds could become victims. In practice this means that they are normally set in tunnels made from wood, stone, drain pipes, earth or whatever may be to hand. Again, they must be inspected daily and only traps approved and licensed by the authorities may be employed. Putting a tunnel over an old-fashioned gin trap does not make it legal to use.

Live catch traps come in three main designs. Cage traps for mink and grey squirrels are simple wire mesh boxes with a spring mechanism to close the entrance once a

A cage trap built on the moor to catch crows.

A different design of bridge trap but it serves the same purpose as the others.

predator has entered the trap, attracted by whatever bait is being used as a lure. The main advantage of cage traps is that any unintended captives can be released without harm. The most likely 'innocent' victims are otters getting into traps set for mink and red squirrels entering grey squirrel traps. There are also live catch traps for rabbits, rats, mice and, at the other end of the scale, foxes, all of which may be of use where particular circumstances make the use of poison (for rats and mice) or snares (for rabbits and foxes) impractical.

Live catch traps for crows come in two designs: one fixed and one portable. The fixed trap is normally a large cage enclosed with wire netting and equipped with some form of inlet that allows a crow to enter the trap but prevents it from flying back out again. This is normally either a funnel like those found in lobster pots, or a horizontal 'ladder' with the rungs spaced at intervals that allow a crow to slip through easily on the way in but that are too narrow for the bird to fly back out. The portable trap, usually called a Larsen trap even when the design is not exactly the same as the original Larsen, is a smaller cage that can be moved around the shoot. A spring-loaded door is held open by a 'perch' that will slip aside and allow the door to slam shut when a crow or magpie lands on it.

In either type of trap the usual 'bait' to attract victims is a live crow or magpie. The law requires that the decoy bird is provided with food, water, shelter and enough space to stretch its wings – all of which it is to be hoped any reasonable keeper would provide in any case. The trap must be checked at least once per day and captured birds must be humanely destroyed. It is not uncommon for non-target species such as hawks and buzzards to get into cage traps – possibly because they see the decoy bird as an easy meal – and they must be released unharmed at the earliest opportunity.

Predator control is an all-year round task for the moorland keeper but as we have already seen it is at its most important in the spring and early summer when the grouse are nesting and rearing their young. The law requires that all traps and snares are inspected daily and on a large area of moorland just getting round all the traps can be a time-consuming business. This can cause problems for the keeper who is expected to rear pheasants or partridges in addition to looking after the grouse. Obviously it is a matter of degree: rearing a few hundred pheasants shouldn't present too many problems: running a hatchery and rearing several thousand birds from day-old to adult is unlikely to sit well with proper predator control on the moor.

While heather management and predator control may be the main aspects of the moorland keeper's work they are far from being the whole of it. They are though the two platforms that provide the foundations for producing a shootable surplus of grouse. First the habitat must be suitable for the birds to survive and secondly the pressure from predation must be reduced as far as is legally possible. Beyond that there are numerous other duties such as dealing with the general public and with various voluntary and regulatory bodies, building and maintaining butts, roads, lunch huts and fences, controlling ticks, organising shooting, carrying out spring and summer grouse counts and controlling the beaters, flankers and pickers-up on shoot days. Some of

Keeper leading a group of beaters along a hill road to the start of the next drive.

these will be covered in the next chapter, Moorland Management, the remainder we will consider here.

Ticks seem to be becoming an increasing menace to the red grouse. They carry diseases such as louping ill that can affect grouse (and Lyme disease that can affect humans) but they can also kill grouse chicks by sheer weight of numbers when the tick population is particularly high. This increase in ticks may be due to a run of mild winters – the 'experts' would no doubt cite global warming – or there may be some other reason, but the effect is the same whatever the cause. A really high tick burden can threaten the very survival of the grouse. Sheep and deer are often blamed for harbouring ticks, though it is debatable if this alone can be the cause since the grouse have shared their habitat with both species for as long as there has been heather moorland managed for shooting.

One recent development in tick control has been to use sheep as 'tick mops'. The idea is to dose the sheep with one of the proprietary tick treatments designed to kill the insects and then move them around the moor so that the ticks which attack the sheep will be killed. It seems to be effective, but requires regular gathering and dosing of the

Picker-up bringing grouse to the game cart at the end of a drive.

sheep, plus some effort being made to ensure that they are not all hefted into a small part of the moor leaving the ticks free to flourish on the rest of the ground. This approach to tick control is generally easier where the sheep are owned by the shoot management but it can be problematic where the grazing rights are not under their direct control. There is little enough money in hill sheep anyway without spending a considerable amount on pesticides principally to benefit the grouse.

One aspect of moorland keepering that has become increasingly important over the past couple of decades is dealing with the public and with various public bodies and quangos such as English Nature, Scottish Natural Heritage, Defra and SEERAD (as the English and Scottish ministries for agriculture etc. are called in their latest manifestations), the RSPB, the Ramblers' Association and local wildlife groups. The days when a keeper might go from one year to the next without seeing anyone apart from his employers and their guests have long gone and today there is a public relations dimension to keepering as well as the more traditional duties. While this development may have been viewed with some trepidation in many quarters in practice most keepers have learned to adapt and even to welcome the increased interest in their work and their workplace.

The Right to Roam legislation introduced at the start of the twenty-first century has not generally had the level of impact that some feared. Though not framed by law as a legal right, most people who wanted to walk the hills and moors of Britain had no difficulty in doing so and provided that they were not deliberately creating a nuisance – by starting fires or allowing their dogs to run wild – were tolerated and encouraged by most keepers and moorland owners.

Giving the public a 'right' to roam over moorland was never likely to result in an explosion of hikers criss-crossing the moors in vast numbers. Most hikers prefer to stick to defined tracks and footpaths where the walking is much easier than striking off across the open moor and where, incidentally, there is much less danger of getting lost. With provisions for denying access on shoot days and restricting it during nesting time, the legislation has probably had little if any negative impact on most moors. The majority of visitors to the countryside are attracted to 'honeypot' sites where there are car parks and facilties such as toilets, tea rooms, souvenir shops and lots of other tourists.

While hikers may do unintentional damage to the grouse, particularly during the nesting season when disturbance and uncontrolled dogs can be a real problem, poachers represent a far greater threat for some moorland keepers, particularly when their ground is close to a large centre of population. The grouse itself may not be the main quarry of the poacher with deer and hares being more attractive to men with rifles or running dogs but that does not make their attentions any less unwelcome. The vast acreages covered by many moors make it difficult for the keeper who cannot be in more than one spot at a time, though the wide-open nature of heather moorland does mean that it is difficult for the poacher to conceal himself and his vehicle.

Coarse grit is put out to help the grouse digest their diet of heather.

Obviously the keeper should seek to have the best possible relationship with his local police force so that help will be available if required. Local residents can also be a great help to the keeper if they keep their eyes and ears open and are prepared to let him know quickly if they see anything suspicious such as strange vehicles heading out onto the moorland tracks. Probably the best deterrence to poachers is the presence of the keeper on the moor. The bigger and better staffed moors clearly have a considerable advantage over the single-handed keeper, particularly if the lone keeper is known to have other interests that keep him away from his ground at particular times – playing or watching football perhaps or indeed taking part in any activity where it is known that he will be otherwise occupied for a specific period.

Deer control is usually the keeper's responsibility. On those Scottish moors where there are large populations of red deer organising the stalking may be more important than looking after the grouse. Conversely, on many moors deer control is limited to the occasional foray after a roe buck in the early morning or evening. In small numbers deer have little or no effect on grouse but once the distinction between grouse moor and deer forest becomes blurred the impact of the deer can be quite detrimental to the grouse. Over-grazing of heather where deer numbers are high, disturbance at nesting time and distributing ticks can all occur and I have been told (though I have never seen it myself) that red deer hinds will actively seek out grouse nests and eat the eggs.

The pattern on the hill provides evidence of a lot of hard work by the keepers on the well-burnt moor.

Where deer stalking is an occasional activity it can be a useful way of spending the early morning and evenings. Sitting quietly and unobtrusively with rifle and binoculars can reveal a lot of activity that would normally be missed by a keeper hurrying about his work. Actually shooting a deer is often something of a bonus. For the keeper/stalker though, where there is a commercial imperative to kill a certain number of deer every season and a sporting requirement to bring a guest rifle within range of a shootable stag stalking often has to take precedence over the requirements of the grouse.

Moorland keepering is often a lonely way of life but it can also be an extremely satisfying profession. Where the low ground keeper, particularly on big commercial shoots, is sometimes little more than a poultry man looking after thousands and thousands of reared pheasants, the moorland keeper is working much more closely with nature. His aim is to produce a surplus of wild birds that can, and indeed must, be cropped both for sport and for the good of the birds themselves. Having created conditions where the grouse can produce a surplus it is important that the surplus be harvested. If not, there is every possibility that disease will strike and kill a far greater proportion of the grouse than would ever fall victim to the Guns.

In addition, the work that the keeper does to encourage the grouse also has enormous benefits for all the other birds that share its unique habitat. Larks and pipits, curlews and lapwings, golden plover and a host of other birds all benefit from the keeper's work. Heather burning ensures that the moors do not revert to scrub woodland and the network of roads and tracks built for the shooting parties provides safe access to the moors for hikers and cyclists. If there were no grouse, or no grouse shooting, then most of our moors would either be planted with foreign softwood trees or be overrun with sheep. In protecting and preserving these wild places the moorland keeper plays a vital part in preserving part of Britain's natural and sporting heritage.

Moorland Management

As already mooted in the previous chapter there is not really a clear distinction between 'moorland keeping' and 'moorland management'. Certain jobs like vermin control are clearly the preserve of the game keeper where others such as financial planning come under the somewhat imprecise classification of management. Where though would you place shoot organisation, grazing management and major expenditure such as chartering a helicopter to spray bracken? They might well be tasks that are carried out by the keeping staff, but whether they should fall into the 'keeping' or the 'management' classification is largely down to the division of labour on any particular shoot. I have therefore made some quite arbitrary decisions about which chapter to include things in and you are quite at liberty to disagree if you wish.

Shoot Organisation

Shoot organisation covers a very wide area from marketing the shoot to supplying flags for the beaters and flankers. Some of the work would be expected to fall within the remit of the keeping staff on the majority of shoots while other jobs would normally be the responsibility of the shoot owner or his factor, but with practically every task there will be moors where the head keeper is responsible for it and others where he is not. In practice it doesn't matter so much who does things as long as someone does them. From now on therefore I will concentrate on what has to be done and leave the question of who is to do it to the individual arrangements on any particular shoot.

The logical place to start as far as organising grouse shooting is concerned is by deciding how many grouse can be shot in each season. As already stated on numerous occasions the red grouse is a wild bird and the shootable surplus in any one year depends entirely on how well – or how badly – the grouse have survived the winter and gone on to breed in the spring and early summer. In theory it is relatively simple to calculate the number that can be shot. You estimate the number of birds on the moor in summer, take away the number of pairs that the moor can support in spring, take away a few more to allow for losses during the winter and the difference is the number that you can shoot – or try to shoot – during August to December. As is so often the case, the theory is simple but the practical application is a little more difficult.

Well wrapped up on a cold March day to go spring grouse counting with a team of pointers.

There is no simple calculation that will tell you the carrying capacity of the moor. It would be extremely useful if it was possible to say with some confidence that (say) one pair of grouse require ten acres of moorland, therefore a 3,500 acre moor can support 350 pairs of grouse in the spring. Such a calculation might well be accurate – for some moors. Some indeed might be able to carry more than one pair per ten acres while others would need more – possibly much, much more - than ten acres per pair. Only local knowledge can say with any degree of accuracy how many pairs of grouse a moor can carry. And even that figure will vary according to factors such as the severity of the winter and the weather in spring plus how well the heather burning has been carried out. But unless you have an idea how many grouse you want to leave behind at the end of the season it is difficult to estimate how many should be shot during the season. And even that presupposes that you have some idea of how many grouse are on the moor when the season starts. Which brings us to the subject of grouse counting.

Grouse Counts

There are two 'seasons' for grouse counting: the spring, when the aim is to see how many grouse have survived the winter, paired off and established themselves on nesting territories, and the summer, when the objective is to see how many offspring paired birds have managed to rear. The spring count gives you an idea of what might be available to shoot come August. 'Might' is the key word here because bad weather at the wrong time can easily ruin the prospects no matter how good things looked in March and April. Given this degree of uncertainty it is reasonable to question the value of spring grouse counts, but they do have a purpose to serve. Plans for the shooting season cannot always be left until the last moment and, although a good stock of adult birds in the spring does not necessarily translate into a bumper crop of young birds in August the converse is nearly always true. If you don't have the birds on the ground in the spring then there will not be much to shoot when the season starts in August. Spring counts therefore are less accurate as a predictor of riches than as a harbinger of probable misery. Even so: distressing though it may be, it is often best to know in advance if there is little prospect of shooting later in the year.

Cock and hen grouse running away from the pointer during a spring grouse count.

Summer counts, in July and August when the chicks are strong on the wing, should provide an accurate assessment of the number of grouse on the moor. Since grouse, whether paired off in spring or protecting their broods in summer, are difficult to find simply by walking the moor the usual method of grouse counting is to hunt the hill with dogs – ideally with pointers or setters, though many moors manage to conduct useful counts with Labradors or spaniels. Often it is a case of making the best of what is on hand.

In spring you count the number of pairs; in summer the size of the broods is important and the ratio of old birds to young. Ideally you should count the same beats every year and keep an accurate record of what grouse are found. Over the years it is possible to build up a picture of the relationship between the number of birds found when counting and the numbers killed when shooting. There are other factors to consider of course such as the level of shooting pressure applied, but after a few years of careful recording it should be possible to get a good idea of how many birds can be shot without harming the prospects for the following years.

Particularly in the summer there are usually plenty of eager dog handlers looking to get their pointers and setters fit for the season or sharpened up for the summer field trials. A useful symbiotic relationship can be formed between the moorland manager wanting to assess his grouse prospects and the handler looking to train his dogs. It is important though from the moorland manager's point of view that the dog trainer understands that he is expected to contribute reliable and accurate figures of the grouse seen in return for access to the moor to train his dogs.

Shoot Planning

Planning shoot days may be a simple enough task on a dogging moor where the shooting is done by the owner and one or two guests. Assuming that there are dogs available, planning a shoot day may involve no more than taking a look at the weather, deciding that today looks like a good day to shoot some grouse and gathering up guns, dogs, lunches, etc. and setting out for the hill. In complete contrast a big driven day may mean organising eight to ten Guns, a loader for each of them, twenty or so beaters, half a dozen flankers, a team of pickers-up, transport for all of the above and quite possibly lunches, evening meals and accommodation for the Guns plus kennels for their dogs. The shot grouse will have to be collected, sorted and hung in the game larder and collection organised with the game dealer, arrangements made for secure storage of the guests' weapons if they are staying overnight and quite possibly a supply of cartridges laid on especially if some of the Guns are from overseas.

How much of this work is done by the keeper, how much by the shoot manager and how much by outsiders such as sporting agents will differ from estate to estate. For example, the Guns on one day may consist of the owner and his friends, all personally invited and all well known over many years. The next time the moor is shot the Guns may have purchased their day shooting through a sporting agent and be complete strangers to the moor with the agent responsible for arranging their transport and accommodation as well as their shooting. On a let day there will normally be at least an indication of how many grouse may be shot and often either a bag limit or an extra price per brace to be paid if more than an agreed number are killed. Where the Guns are guests of the owner such restrictions are unlikely to be applied.

Planning for the season means starting with an estimate of how many grouse can be shot without eating into the breeding stock, then translating this into 'X' number of days shooting. This may have well have to be re-thought if the early estimates of grouse numbers are wrong and some days cancelled or, if the estimates were too conservative, extra days added. Then shoot dates have to be set, usually in conjunction with the neighbouring moors so that clashes are avoided.

As already indicated, a driven grouse shoot requires a considerable number of people in order to get the grouse over the Guns. Unfortunately for the shoot organiser grouse moors tend to be found in some of the least populated parts of the country and finding sufficient experienced people to ensure that the day runs smoothly can be a difficult task. Normally the keepers from neighbouring moors all help out on each others' shoot days and many of the beaters, loaders and pickers-up will also travel from moor to moor. If two or three moors all arrange driven days for the same date it may be difficult if not impossible for enough bodies to be recruited for all of them. Loading and picking up are specialist jobs that can only be done by experienced people. New recruits can do a good job in the beating line, provided they are fit enough and follow instructions, but there still have to be at least a sprinkling of experienced hands to keep the others right.

In advance of a shoot day – preferably well in advance, though the evening before may well be spent making frantic phone calls – the following arrangements should be in place. The Guns should know where and when to meet, whether they will be shooting single or double guns (and if the latter whether they are to supply their own loaders) and roughly how many cartridges they may require. There is nothing worse than standing in a butt with an empty cartridge bag while covey after covey glides past. Your host will not be too pleased either. The beaters, flankers, pickers-up and loaders should know where and when to congregate and whether they are expected to bring their own lunches or if a lunch will be provided.

Transport has to be arranged for everybody. Many moorland roads are only suitable for four-wheel drive vehicles and it is no use discovering on the morning of the shoot that there is not enough capacity to get everyone into their allotted places. It is not just the number of people that have to be considered when sorting out transport. Dogs, lunches, coats and leggings, guns, cartridge bags and all the other paraphernalia that is needed on a shoot day has to be moved from meet to moor as well.

Many shoots will have transport available for those who don't have suitable vehicles of their own. Such things as tractors and trailers or horse boxes with straw bales for seats can accommodate good numbers though care has to be taken to ensure that there are no breaches of health and safety regulations. These seem to vary from place to place and in any case change with some regularity. While the obvious course of action if in doubt about what is legal would seem to be to check with your local H&S office I would suggest that you think carefully before doing this. Where no clear guidance exists some H&S officers have a tendency to make up policy on the hoof – and there is no guarantee that what they decide will be sensible or practical. However, once H&S have pronounced you ignore them at your peril.

The British Association for Shooting & Conservation (BASC) provides sensible guidance on trailer safety on its website (basc.org.uk). In practice this is mostly common sense – don't let passengers stand up or ride with their legs swinging over the sides; ensure that seats are firmly fixed and that the trailer has a head board and a tail board; keep dogs on leads; have a safe means of getting on and off, and make sure that all this isn't negated by letting some idiot drive too quickly. If you are going on a public road then the trailer must be road legal and have rear lights, indicators and working brakes and your shoot insurance should cover both driver and passengers.

It is possible to buy ex-army trucks and cross-country vehicles specially adapted for transporting guns and beaters and these usually have good ground clearance, proper seating and often four-wheel drive. They are not particularly expensive and may well prove a better alternative for many shoots than making do with whatever farm trailers happen to be available on shoot days or trusting that enough of the beaters, Guns, loaders, etc. will have vehicles suitable for traversing moorland roads and tracks.

An ex-army truck converted to make an excellent transporter for the beaters.

If you anticipate shooting any number of grouse some form of game cart will also be necessary. In hot weather game can deteriorate very quickly, especially if it is slung in a heap on the floor of a trailer and trampled over by boots and paws. Shot grouse should be hung up or laid in trays where they can cool naturally and are protected from flies and the direct heat of the sun. If you are shooting over dogs and anticipate a bag of ten brace or so it is relatively easy to handle the shot birds – indeed, you may have to carry them in a gamebag until you get back to the game larder – but where the bag is likely to run into hundreds you will need some means of handling them all so as to keep them in the best possible condition. Plastic trays can be bought quite cheaply or may be supplied by your game dealer and can be easily washed down after use. Some will self-stack, or you may prefer to fit some sort of shelving arrangement to a vehicle or trailer that the trays can be slid into and held securely.

As with so many other activities, a properly planned and efficiently organised shoot day will appear to run itself. Like any large operation it is essential that everyone knows who is in charge of what: who is responsible for getting the guns and the loaders into the right butts at the right time, who is organising the beating line, who is placing the pickers-up during the drives and coordinating with the guns afterwards to ensure, as far

A well-made game cart designed to keep the shot grouse in good condition until they reach the game larder.

Grouse are laid in trays and then slotted into the cart so the air can circulate around them.

Using an Argocat to ferry the Guns out to their butts.

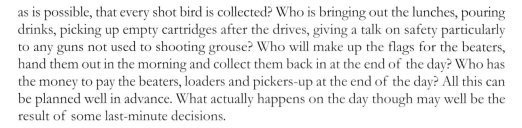

as is possible, that every shot bird is collected? Who is bringing out the lunches, pouring drinks, picking up empty cartridges after the drives, giving a talk on safety particularly to any guns not used to shooting grouse? Who will make up the flags for the beaters, hand them out in the morning and collect them back in at the end of the day? Who has the money to pay the beaters, loaders and pickers-up at the end of the day? All this can be planned well in advance. What actually happens on the day though may well be the result of some last-minute decisions.

Shoot Day Organisation

Assuming that you have some grouse to shoot the most important factor influencing any shoot day is likely to be the weather. Mist, fog or heavy rain may mean that the day has to be cut short or cancelled entirely, but even when the sun shines from a clear sky on a shoot morning there may have to be some late changes to the plan. With grouse – and especially driven grouse – the strength and direction of the wind will have a considerable influence on how a shoot day is organised.

It is quite normal when driving grouse to bring in vast acreages of moorland in an attempt to concentrate the birds so that eventually they fly over a relatively short line of butts. This is done by a combination of beaters and flankers who get the birds on the wing and then try to funnel them into the area where the guns are waiting. With the wind in the right direction this may by quite straightforward; with the wind in the wrong direction it may be close to impossible. The first requirement for a shoot day is an accurate weather forecast. The second requirement is that someone has the experience to understand what effect the wind will have on the way the grouse will fly.

Driving grouse is rather more complicated than simply sending the birds from one beat over one set of butts. It is normal to use one drive to fill up another. Having flown through the butts on one drive and settled in the heather on another beat the grouse can often be picked up on another drive and sent over the guns a second time. Obviously the layout of every moor will differ as will the way the grouse behave, but under the right conditions it is often possible – and indeed essential if enough birds are to be shot – to show many of the same birds to the guns two or three times in one shoot day. However, for this to work it is essential that someone has the knowledge and experience not only to predict how the grouse are likely to fly in any particular combination of wind and weather but also to be able to adapt to events if the grouse don't elect to follow the plan.

Of course, the objective may not always be to show the maximum number of birds to the Guns. If for example a well-stocked grouse moor has arranged for a team of guns to shoot a relatively modest number of birds it may be better to arrange the drives so that the birds are only shown to the Guns once or to reduce the area that is brought in for each drive. That way a full day's shooting should be possible without going way over the bag limit and either saddling the Guns with a much higher bill than antici-pated or having to stop shooting at lunchtime.

Too many birds may not be the problem. Grouse can be quite contrary at times and despite the wind being in the perfect direction and the best efforts of the beaters and flankers they may swing back or off to the side and either miss the line of butts or settle in the wrong part of the moor for later drives. At this stage there are some delicate decisions to be made. Do you carry on with the original plan and hope that things get better, or do you hatch an entirely new strategy and put it into effect on the hoof? Either way may result in triumph or disaster and the only way to find out which of Kipling's 'two imposters' it might be is to go ahead with one plan or the other and hope you've guessed correctly. Sometimes running a shoot day is simple and straightforward; sometimes it isn't.

While nothing will be more important to the success of the day than getting grouse over Guns there are all sorts of little touches that can make the day more enjoyable and more memorable for the Guns whether they are guests or clients. Ensuring that there is a strong dog tether at every butt is as easy as hammering in a stout post but it can be a great help to the Gun with a dog that is less than perfectly steady. A dram or a shot of sloe gin between drives, nicely presented in proper glasses, will cost only a few pounds but it creates a favourable impression – provided your Guns are not of a religious belief that prohibits alcohol. Game markers for noting the fall of each grouse help the pickers-up as well as the Guns; a clean, dry and tidy lunch hut, clearly numbered and well-maintained butts that are not littered with ancient cartridges rusting away, and roads that are not riddled with pot holes all help to reinforce the feeling that the moor is well run, the shoot properly organised and that the enjoyment of the Guns is paramount. They are, after all, the whole reason for everyone else being present and, on many shoots, it is only the money paid by the Guns on let days that enables the shoot to continue at all. Look after your Guns as well as you can – and then look after everyone else involved with the shoot with just as much regard for their comfort and feelings. It will more than pay you back in the long term.

Habitat Improvements

It is hard not to feel a certain irony when considering the various ways in which it may be possible to improve moorland habitat. Not too many years ago the government would pay grants in order to assist landowners to 'improve' heather moorland by liming and re-seeding the ground in order to kill off the heather and replace it with grass for sheep and cattle to graze. Sometimes quite reasonable pasture resulted but often the 'improved' ground simply turned into a sour, boggy morass of rushes and white grass that was less use for grazing than the heather it replaced. Today under the various schemes run by the government it may be possible to claim grants that will help to bring back heather on some of the 'improved' grazings.

Another way of improving heather moorland that was popular a few years ago was to cut drains to run water off the hill. In practice draining did little to improve the heather but often had a detrimental effect on the grouse. Grouse chicks following their mother were liable to drop into the drains and, if there was any amount of water flowing they were quickly washed away and either drowned or died from the cold and wet. Recent thinking would suggest that draining was actually detrimental for the grouse – even those that didn't drown – because the very wet areas that were being drained were both a source of water in dry summers and a breeding ground for some of the insects that are vital to grouse chicks in the first couple of weeks of their lives. On many moors now drains are allowed to silt up or deliberately blocked to allow bogs and wet patches to reform.

Heather is a resilient plant and in many cases will regenerate naturally simply by removing grazing pressure. This can be seen quite clearly where parts of a hill where heather was apparently barely clinging on to existence are fenced off for planting with trees. With deer and sheep excluded from the ground the heather will often regenerate in spectacular fashion at least until it is smothered by the trees. Where moorland has been supplanted with grazing on a large scale it is often possible to return it to heather by reseeding the ground though doing this over a large enough acreage to make a noticeable difference to grouse numbers is likely to be an expensive project.

Well managed heather on the left: over-grazed ground reverting to rough grass on the other side of the fence.

The boundary between the heather moorland and the 'improved' grazing is clear to see on this Cumbrian fell.

One weed that can be eradicated – though again, not cheaply – is bracken. Bracken can spread remarkably quickly and not only takes over from the heather but harbours ticks and can poison grazing animals. If you only have a small area and wish to stop it spreading before it can get out of hand it may be possible to kill it off with a hand sprayer or one mounted on the back of a quad bike, but really large areas of bracken call for more radical solutions. Employing a helicopter to spray the bracken will cost a lot of money but may well be more cost effective than spending many man-hours trying to kill it off with slower and less effective spraying techniques. A helicopter can spray bracken just about anywhere it is growing, no matter how steep or how rocky the ground, nor how far it is from the nearest vehicular access.

Bracken can also be killed by crushing it with a roller when it is first sprouting, though this will have to be repeated at least once when the bracken re-emerges. In order for the bracken to die off completely the process will have to be repeated, possibly over several years. Where the bracken is growing in an area that allows access with a tractor the type of swipe used to cut fire breaks when heather burning can be used to cut the bracken back while it is in the early stages of growth. Where the bracken is growing on marginal ground it may not be necessary to try and eradicate it altogether provided that the edges are sprayed, crushed or cut so as to prevent it steadily creeping further and further into the heather.

Hill Grazing

The two animals most likely to be found grazing on heather moorland are sheep and deer. There are differing opinions about the value to a grouse moor of both species, but there is no doubt that over-grazing by either species is severely detrimental to the heather and to the grouse. The important phrase in that sentence is, of course 'over-grazing'.

If there are too many sheep, too many deer or possibly an excess of both species there is no question that the heather will suffer and the grouse will suffer as a consequence. Too many grazing animals eat down the heather and encourage the growth of other species such as grasses that take over from it. Too many sharp hooves in combination with vegetation that is nibbled down to the roots can also cause erosion and the disturbance from sheep, shepherds and sheep dogs will not be welcome especially during the nesting season.

That said, it is generally agreed that most heather moors will benefit from a reasonable amount of grazing to help keep grasses and shrubs from invading the heather, though there may be some disagreement as to what constitutes 'reasonable' as far as grazing heather is concerned. As already discussed, sheep can be used as 'tick mops' to try to control the number of ticks that spread conditions such as louping ill and Lyme disease. Indeed, some pundits attribute the rise in tick-borne disease to the fact that sheep numbers have been drastically reduced or removed altogether on many hills and moors.

Sheep and deer do have an economic contribution to make towards the moorland accounts and in some cases may be the only way of making the moor financially viable. Sheep generate cash from meat, wool and subsidies, and it is probably true that in recent years the subsidies have been of far more importance than either meat or wool in making moorland sheep pay their way. As I write this there are very real concerns about the future viability of sheep farming in Britain. Another foot and mouth outbreak – this time emanating from a government controlled laboratory – has meant that hill lamb exports are banned, and bluetongue disease has spread into the south-east of England and looks likely to spread north and west over the next year or so. It is impossible to forecast what may happen in both the short and long term as regards subsidies, export opportunities and market values for sheep but whatever the future holds it will certainly impact on grouse moor managers as well as on farmers and shepherds.

Deer can also contribute to the profitability of moorland through venison sales and stalking fees, though there may be difficulties reconciling the different requirements of stalkers and grouse shooters particularly during September and October. Much will depend on whether the moor is best described as a deer forest with some grouse or as a grouse moor with some deer. Stalkers want to see as little disturbance as possible on the hill so that the deer are calm and settled and this doesn't fit well with driving grouse where the beating line will send every deer on the place scampering across the march.

Walking up will have much the same effect and even shooting over dogs, where fewer people are involved, will still clear large areas of deer.

It is said that in the past, particularly in the Highlands, some stalkers would deliberately trample any grouse nests that they found since a grouse exploding out of the heather and alerting a stag spells sure ruination to a stalk. Nowadays, with grouse numbers drastically reduced on many Highland estates it is unlikely that even the keenest stalker would deliberately destroy a nest. Even just a few coveys that offer the chance of a day or two shooting over dogs will provide a handy source of revenue or a day or two's diversion for the owner of the ground.

Income and Expenditure

Calculating the cash flow for a grouse moor is a much more problematic exercise than doing the same thing for a pheasant or partridge shoot. On most low ground shoots the number of birds that can be shot in any one season is directly related to the number of birds that are released. Certainly things can go wrong – predation or disease can spoil the best laid plans – but in general, if the shoot manager decides that (say) four

A well built lunch hut allows the shooting party to dine in comfort whatever the weather.

thousand pheasants should be shot, he can extrapolate that, given a forty per cent return, he needs to budget for ten thousand poults to be released. All other calculations as to the cost of keepering, rearing, feeding, etc. can be forecast with reasonable accuracy, a cash flow forecast produced and a profit and loss statement calculated and waved at the bank manager when the ongoing overdraft is discussed. The grouse moor manager enjoys no such certainty.

True he can predict certain costs with reasonable accuracy. Rent, rates, keepers' wages, housing and vehicle costs will be pretty much the same year on year. There may be capital projects that impact on the budget – driving new roads across the moor, building a new lunch hut or a new line of butts – but unless an extra keeper is employed, or a keepering position is made redundant the non-capital expenditure will be much the same year after year, apart from the variable costs by which I mean the cost of employing beaters, pickers-up, flankers and the like on shooting days.

Again, on a low ground shoot these costs would be more or less fixed from year to year. It doesn't matter whether you are a small syndicate shooting once a fortnight through November to January or a big commercial setup planning a hundred or more let days at partridges and pheasants starting on the first of September. As long as you know how often you will be shooting you can predict your variable costs with reasonable accuracy. On a grouse moor though things are completely different. Until probably the middle of July or even a week or two later you won't be able to forecast the cost of beaters etc. because you won't know how many days – if any – you will be shooting.

But the really big problem for the grouse moor owner aiming to produce a cash flow forecast, as any good businessman should, is not that it is difficult to assess costs accurately but that it is almost impossible to forecast what the income will be – if there is any income at all.

Grouse numbers are variable in any case with good years and bad years occurring roughly according to a cyclical pattern. Most moors have a pretty fair idea of the maximum number of birds that they might shoot in a really excellent year, and every moor owner knows exactly how many can be shot in a really bad one. None at all. The problem is to know where in the cycle you are likely to be in any one year. This is not just important for assessing costs but vital for knowing how much income – if any income at all – is likely to be received.

If there are few grouse and no shooting then the income will be zero: there will be no need to find money for the variable costs such as beaters, but the rest of the outlay – keepers' wages, rents, maintenance costs, insurance, vehicle and housing costs and so on – will still have to be met. There may be a contribution from the sheep or the stalking, but in a very bad year running a grouse moor is all about paying out with little or nothing coming in to defray the expenditure. It is a very different matter from running a low ground shoot where income is largely dependent on the number of birds released – a factor totally in the control of the shoot management.

There are some compensations to offset this. The current cost of shooting a brace of grouse is, at around £120 to £140, approximately double or even treble the £50 or

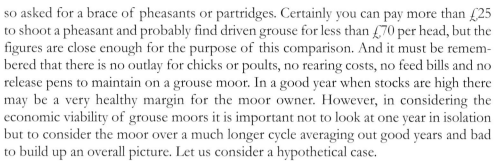

so asked for a brace of pheasants or partridges. Certainly you can pay more than £25 to shoot a pheasant and probably find driven grouse for less than £70 per head, but the figures are close enough for the purpose of this comparison. And it must be remembered that there is no outlay for chicks or poults, no rearing costs, no feed bills and no release pens to maintain on a grouse moor. In a good year when stocks are high there may be a very healthy margin for the moor owner. However, in considering the economic viability of grouse moors it is important not to look at one year in isolation but to consider the moor over a much longer cycle averaging out good years and bad to build up an overall picture. Let us consider a hypothetical case.

Suppose we have a moor – say seven or eight thousand acres of good heather – that can produce a crop of fifteen hundred brace of grouse in really good year. At £140 per brace that would amount to over £200,000. Allow £60,000 for two keepers and their associated costs, perhaps £20,000 for rent, another £20,000 for maintenance and you have a gross margin of £100,000. Assume that there are ten days' shooting in a good year, averaging 150 brace, and that you hire twenty beaters, ten flankers and half a dozen pickers-up for each day at £25 per head – call it £10,000. That leaves you with a £90,000 margin, plus whatever you get for the shot grouse. Let's call it a round £100,000. Now consider what your margin will be in a really bad year. This is quite straightforward: it is all the fixed costs with no variable costs and no income, i.e. a loss of £100,000. And if you are hit by disease immediately after that bumper year (which is quite likely to happen) all the accumulated profit will be wiped out. Completely. Perhaps sinking your life savings into a grouse moor isn't such a sound investment after all?

A good picker-up will repay the cost of employing them many times over.

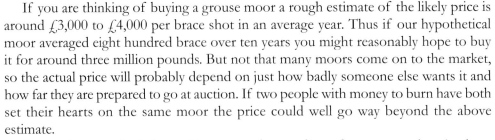

If you are thinking of buying a grouse moor a rough estimate of the likely price is around £3,000 to £4,000 per brace shot in an average year. Thus if our hypothetical moor averaged eight hundred brace over ten years you might reasonably hope to buy it for around three million pounds. But not that many moors come on to the market, so the actual price will probably depend on just how badly someone else wants it and how far they are prepared to go at auction. If two people with money to burn have both set their hearts on the same moor the price could well go way beyond the above estimate.

In practice any calculations of income and expenditure from grouse shooting have to look at a period of several years and average out the fluctuations in numbers shot. Over a long time – fifty or a hundred years – there is a reasonably regular cycle of around six years between peaks and troughs in grouse population numbers, but in the short term the regularity of the cycle is skewed by factors such as the weather. Bad weather at hatching time or an exceptionally severe winter could easily ruin what should have been a bumper year, while an exceptionally good spring and early summer might go some way to alleviating the shortage of grouse anticipated at the bottom of a cycle. Overall though, it is essential to put aside some of the income from a good year because there is little doubt that a bad year will follow sooner or later.

Just because it is difficult to calculate income from a moor does not mean that there is no merit in producing cash flow predictions and profit and loss forecasts. If nothing else is achieved at least it will help to concentrate your mind (and possibly your bank manager's mind) on the reality of grouse moor management, which we might sum up as offering the potential to make a reasonable return on outlay occasionally and the near certainty of plunging into deficit at regular intervals. It is certainly not a sound investment to anyone who hopes to rely on it to produce a regular income and generate sufficient cash each year to cover their expenditure.

I am writing as if the prime consideration of moorland management were commercial, but I realise that this is often not the case. Many moors are run mainly or exclusively for the enjoyment of the owner/tenant and their guests with no intention of generating sufficient income to offset the cost of managing the moor, though clearly this approach to financial management requires a considerable input from outside resources. Probably the majority of moors are run along lines that are neither fully commercial nor fully philanthropic, with some shooting days being enjoyed by the owner and guests and some days let out to help offset the costs of running the moor. Whatever the balance between sport and commerce it can be interesting to look at the annual outlay and compare it with the notional amount that could have been earned if all the shooting had been sold at whatever the current price per brace might be. If nothing else it will give you an idea of what the commercial potential of your sport would be if you ever decided to realise it in full.

There are other calculations that may be of interest to the moorland manager. If we take the cost of running a day's driven shooting as estimated above – approximately £1,000 per day – and divide it by the price charged for shooting a brace of grouse – say

Good hill roads are expensive to build and maintain but they are a real boon on shooting days.

£140 – we can calculate that it only requires about eight brace of grouse to be shot to cover the cost of employing those beaters and flankers. Roughly speaking, one brace of grouse will cover the wages of four or five beaters, which would suggest that skimping on labour is likely to be false economy. A picker-up has only to find one grouse that would otherwise have been lost to more than cover the cost of his employment. Bearing in mind how hard it can be to collect every shot bird it is probably true that the more pickers-up you can deploy the better.

What about the cost of predation to the moor owner? Suppose that a fox manages to kill half a dozen nesting hen grouse, and suppose that each of those nests might have produced eight grouse chicks to grow up and fly over the Guns on a shoot day. At £140 per brace that equates to £3,360. Even if we assume that only half of those forty-eight young grouse feature in the bag that fox has still cost us the thick end of £2,000. And that is without projecting forward to the next year and how many, if any, chicks the surviving grouse might have produced. Predators are an expensive luxury on a grouse moor. A pheasant shoot could replace that hypothetical loss of fifty or so poults by buying in another fifty – total outlay perhaps £150. Predation on a grouse moor is far more expensive and totally irrecoverable.

Walked up days are generally much cheaper to organise since the Guns themselves, with their own dogs, play the role of beaters and quite possibly supply their own lunches. In some cases the only direct expense to the estate will be the cost of a day's wages for the keeper who accompanies them to organise and direct the line of Guns. This is not always so of course and a walked up day could involve beaters with dogs interspersed between the walking Guns, and even one or two people with retrievers specifically for picking-up, though they would not normally be needed unless the Guns had no dogs at all with them. Birds shot while walking in line are usually picked immediately with little question about how many have been shot or where exactly the birds fell. There may be exceptions where a pricked bird flies a considerable distance before dropping and at times like this someone who can be detached from the line to go to the fall will stand a good chance of picking a bird that would otherwise be lost. And if the guns are paying £80 per brace for their walked up day, that one bird will easily cover the costs of employing the picker-up.

Hiring a team of pointers and setters for a day over dogs at around £150 or more per day, plus travelling expenses, may seem expensive when compared to the costs of beaters at £25 to £35 per head but a good team of birddogs plus a retriever is all that is needed to provide a full day's sport. Guns who appreciate good dog work and who like to feel that they have earned their sport in a physical as well as financial sense should be willing to pay a reasonable wage to the dog team that supplies them. The season for

Hot and smoky work carrying out the heather burning plan.

shooting grouse over dogs is limited to a few brief weeks in August and September but the dogs have to be kennelled, fed, trained and exercised all year round. If your team of birddogs plus handler cost £200 and the guns are paying £80 per brace it only takes three brace to move you into profit. A ten brace day – easily achievable if you have even a few grouse on the moor – would show an income of four times your outlay: a respectable return in almost any business.

In recent years some moor owners have begun releasing partridges on the less productive areas of their ground in order to guarantee some sport in years when the grouse population is too low to allow much if any shooting. Provided that looking after the partridges does not take up too many hours of keepering time at the expense of the work that is required for the grouse this can provide a little shooting and possibly some income in poor seasons without having any impact on the grouse prospects. Partridges can be released on ground where no grouse will normally be found – bracken, rushes, rough grazing and scrubby woodland – but they can also thrive on the heather itself. A few partridges should have no effect at all on grouse prospects either from the point of view of diverting resources from moorland management or the risk of spreading disease or parasites to the grouse. However, to release several thousand partridges onto the most productive areas of the moor would not seem like a sensible move for both the above reasons.

Heather moorland is a unique and delicate environment that may look wild and entirely natural but is generally only created and maintained by a lot of hard work. Left to itself most moorland will revert to scrubby woodland where it lies below the tree line. Where heather is not burnt it becomes long and rank and of little value to grouse or grazing animals. Bracken, rush and other invasive plants can take over and kill off large acreages of heather if left unchecked. Where moorland is not managed for grouse it often becomes over-grazed by sheep, cattle or deer or suffers the final act of destruction when it is turned over to commercial forestry. The great moorland expanses of Northern England, Scotland, Wales and Ireland may appear vast and indestructible but in fact they represent only a fraction of the acreage of moorland that existed a century ago.

Some wildlife enthusiasts and conservationists will argue that grouse moor management is aimed at preserving a monoculture of heather with the aim of increasing the population of a single species to the detriment of many others, and there is an element of truth in this argument. A grouse moor is not a true 'natural' environment, but neither is practically any other part of the British Isles. The hand of Man and the changes he has made both by accident and by design can be seen practically everywhere from the Channel Islands to the Shetlands and all points in between. Certainly the preservation of the red grouse is the primary reason for all the work that is carried out on the moor, but many other species benefit directly and indirectly from this. Some do not: predators such as foxes and crows are targeted directly, and those species of birds, animals and plants that would thrive if the heather were allowed to revert to scrub and woodland are disadvantaged by default. Equally, birds of the open moors such as larks, pipits, curlews and peewits benefit both from the environment that is created and maintained for the grouse and from the lack of predation that allows them to nest and raise their broods.

Managing a grouse moor is unlikely to make a fortune for the owner. Rather the prospective grouse moor proprietor would be well advised to make his fortune first and then buy a grouse moor as a means of redistributing his wealth. The financial side of moorland management is easy to summarise. In a good year there *may* be a considerable margin to enter in the profit side of the ledger; in a bad year there *will* be a considerable loss.

The total outlay can be relatively modest where it is limited mainly to the costs of keepering staff or it can be astronomical where new roads are driven through the moor, helicopters are brought in to spray bracken, 'improved' grazings are re-seeded, and other capital projects are undertaken. There are any number of ways to spend money on a grouse moor and no guarantee that there will be any return whatsoever as far as grouse shooting is concerned. Indeed, it is almost certain that there will be years where the grouse population crashes and no shooting at all can take place.

Against that, there will, hopefully, be years when there are plenty of grouse and enough shooting to satisfy both the sporting and commercial aspirations of the moorland manager. In addition there is the satisfaction of helping to preserve an increasingly rare and uniquely British habitat, of providing some of the best shooting available anywhere in the world, of continuing a tradition of sport that has been followed for over three hundred years and of living and working in a landscape that is both beautiful and challenging in equal measure.

There are many worse ways of making a living.

Taking Part

Grouse shooting is the same as any other sport in that there is no substitute for taking part. You can read about it, watch documentaries on television, buy video tapes and DVDs showing how it is done and dream about it in idle moments, but nothing can replace the feel of the moorland wind in your face, the smell of peat dust and pollen, the feel of rock and heather under your boots and the sight of a pointer quartering the hill, a beating line tramping through the heather or a covey of grouse gliding, turning, rising and falling as they approach the butts.

In one sense the only way to experience the sights, sounds and smells of a day shooting grouse is to take part yourself. Grouse shooting is not a spectator sport. It would be difficult and dangerous to try to arrange for a gallery at a driven grouse shoot. Difficult, because the sight of a crowd of spectators would almost certainly influence the flight of the grouse, and dangerous because, unless the watchers were standing a long, long way from the Guns they stand a very real chance of being peppered by shot. It would not even be feasible for them to stand well behind the butts equipped with binoculars because they would possibly be spoiling the next drive by preventing the grouse from dropping into the heather from where they would later be flushed back over the Guns.

Certainly some spectators will be found on many driven days but the usual place to find them is in the butts alongside a partner, friend or relative getting a close-up view of the action. The only safe place in the immediate area of the Guns on a driven grouse shoot is in or alongside one of the butts – and even then there is always a risk of a neighbour swinging through the line. Fortunately there is little demand for ringside seats on a grouse moor – other perhaps than for photographers looking for pictures to illustrate books and magazine articles. The obvious way to take part is as a Gun shooting driven grouse, walking up or shooting over pointing dogs but to do so requires either friends in the right places (i.e. friends who own grouse moors) or quite a bit of cash to spare. There is though ample scope for anyone who wants to get a closer look at driven grouse shooting without spending a lot of money simply by volunteering to help out – as a beater, flanker, loader or picker-up.

Of the four jobs listed it is that of beater that lends itself best to the employment of unskilled labour. This is not to suggest that working as a beater on a grouse moor

Beaters taking a well-earned rest between drives.

is easy: only that it is less skilled (though possible more demanding physically) than the other three tasks.

The beaters' job is to get grouse on the wing and moving in the direction of the Guns waiting in the butts. This is normally done by waving a flag – 'snapping'a flag might be a more accurate description – while marching quite quickly in line with the other beaters. No experience or local knowledge is necessary since there will be a keeper (or several keepers) to issue instructions and speak to you in low, dulcet tones if you don't keep your rightful place in the line. What is required is a reasonable level of physical fitness, the ability to walk quite a few miles at a reasonable pace over rough moorland and arms that can swing and snap a flag while so doing. The flag will normally be supplied.

There is no particular dress code for beaters either. While a loader would certainly not be welcome in a butt dressed in a white tee shirt there is no reason why a beater should not set out clad thus: indeed, it might even be an advantage given that the aim of the beaters is to get grouse on the wing by appearing as a visible threat to the birds. A tee shirt might not be the ideal garment on wet or windy days but on a hot August afternoon a pair of shorts and a light top will be a lot more comfortable than the thick tweed suit, collar and tie that a 'properly' dressed beater might be wearing.

Proper footwear is important though, particularly where the ground is steep, rocky or boggy – all or any of which conditions can be found on most grouse moors. It doesn't matter that your shoes are waterproof – provided that you don't mind getting wet feet – since most grouse shooting takes place in summer or early autumn when there is little danger of frostbite, but it is essential that the soles of your shoes or boots have a good enough grip to prevent you slipping and sliding all over the place. A set of lightweight waterproofs is always useful to have along, plus something to drink on hot days. Other than that you can pretty much please yourself as to your mode of dress and provided you stay in line and keep waving your flag you have every chance of being asked back again.

Flanking is a rather more skilled job than beating though it will normally not involve quite so much physical effort. The flankers' job is to help funnel the grouse over the Guns as they approach the butts and to stop them from leaking out at the edges of the drive. In theory this is fairly simple: the flanker is equipped with a flag which he or she waves at any covey that looks like exiting the drive without crossing the line of Guns. In theory the sight of the flag will turn the grouse and they will cross the line of Guns as intended. In practice flanking requires a little bit more from its exponents than simply waving a flag. The timing of the wave can be quite important.

Good flanking is more of an art than a science. A drive may start out with the beaters covering a front of half a mile or more across and end up at a line of Guns that extends

An eager Labrador poses on the top of a butt as he waits to be sent for a retrieve.

perhaps two or three hundred yards from one end to the other. If the drive goes according to plan the grouse should be moved forward and inwards so that they all – or nearly all – end up flying over the waiting Guns. Moving them forwards may be easy enough at the start of the drive but as they are moved further and further from their home territories they become more and more liable to swing off to left or right or to try and swing back over the beating line. The flankers are there to turn the birds that edge off to the sides back into the centre of the drive.

If the flags are waved too early they may have the opposite of the desired effect and turn the grouse back away from the Guns. If they are left too late before being shown the grouse may be committed to their course and ignore them. Get the timing just right and the grouse should swing away from the flankers towards the Guns. At least that is the theory, and if the wind isn't too strong, or the grouse too determined that is what will happen. Some of the time. The measure of a good flanker is that they will put more grouse over the butts than a bad flanker, but even with the best and most experienced exponent of the art there will be grouse and coveys of grouse that simply ignore the flag and swing off to safety on the right or the left of the line. With luck they may be caught up in a later drive and if not, well, there is usually another day and if not enough birds have to be left for breeding stock.

There is no strict division of labour between flankers and beaters and it is quite likely that someone who is beating on one drive could be asked to act as a flanker on another. Much depends on the terrain and the way in which a moor is driven. On some drives a flanker may have to link up with the beaters as they reach his position and continue with them to the end of the drive, while other beats may see the flankers staying in a fixed position until the drive is over. It all depends on the moor, the way the grouse normally fly and the experience and instinct of the head keeper. Alternating beaters and flankers can also be a way of spreading the work load and allowing some of the older or less fit beaters to have a bit of a break, especially when the weather is hot and the going is hard.

Pickers-up and loaders, in contrast to beaters and flankers, tend to be used only in the role for which they are employed. The main requirement for the picker-up on a grouse shoot is a good dog or even better a team of good dogs. As discussed in earlier chapters, one of the most difficult things about driven grouse shooting is to collect all the shot birds. A dog can earn its keep and more than repay the wages of a picker-up for a day just by retrieving a single grouse.

The place for a picker-up on a driven grouse shoot while the drive is under way is well back behind the Guns. Very, very well back, because there is liable to be a lot of lead in the air behind the butts and a dog or a picker-up who is stationed too close is at risk of collecting some of it. Being stationed well back also helps the picker-up to spot those grouse that have been pricked by shot but not dropped immediately and those that have got a leg down but are still capable of flying. Pricked birds will often fly quite a distance before dropping and it is not unusual for grouse that the Gun may have thought had been missed completely to suddenly drop dead in the heather. The

A Gun and his loader accompanied by a spaniel on their way to the butts.

first task of the picking-up team is to collect these birds and any wounded ones that can be retrieved.

Provided that you are far enough back to be completely safe from a stray shot, and provided that you are confident that your dog will not take off to join in the action around the butts, it makes sense to try and pick pricked and wounded birds as quickly as possible even though the drive is still going on. A wounded grouse can run for a considerable distance if its legs are not damaged, or tuck down into the heather where it is difficult for a dog to find it and the sooner your dog is on the scent the better the chances that the bird will be found. Once the drive ends and the grouse that dropped well back have been collected the pickers-up go forward to help in the main gather of birds that dropped around the butts.

It is at this stage that confusion often reigns. Some of the beaters may have dogs that have lifted birds as the line reaches the butts or they may themselves have picked up any grouse that they spot lying in the heather. Then the Guns, the loaders or any companions watching the shooting may have their own dogs working or have picked dead birds themselves. And there may be some confusion about exactly how many grouse are down, where they fell, whether they were dead or runners and whether they have already been picked or not. Your job as a picker-up is to try and make sense of all this and then collect every shot bird – or at least as many as possible.

Picker-up with a well trained team of Labradors.

If you are lucky the Gun, loader or admiring spectator will have kept a count of what fell and where. This will not be the final word on where birds will be picked because a grouse with a broken wing that crumples and crashes to the ground 'stone dead' may well have run as soon as it could get to its feet and gather its senses. At least though, you should have an idea of how many birds you are looking for and roughly where you might expect to find them. At some stage the Guns and beaters will drift away towards the next drive leaving some or all of the pickers-up to continue searching. The search will probably end up with a grand sweep all round the line of butts and then the picking-up team will head off to take up their posts behind the butts for the next drive.

There is often a call for a picker-up when the Guns are shooting over dogs. This is liable to involve a lot more walking than when picking-up on a driven shoot since the picker-up has to go wherever the shooting party goes. Provided you are fit enough to enjoy a long walk over the moor this can be a relaxed and informal way to spend a day and excellent training for a young dog. The picker-up stays in the background while the pointers or setters quarter the hill and point the grouse. Once the Guns go forward to the point and – assuming they are successful – a grouse or two or three has been dropped into the heather the pointing dogs will be told to 'Hup!' (lie down) and the retrievers can come forward to do their job.

Usually you will know exactly what is to be picked and more or less where it fell, though there may be exceptions when a grouse is known to have been pricked but still flies a long way off before pitching into the heather. When this happens, unless it has dropped in at a spot where the pointers will be quartering shortly afterwards, the picker-up is liable to be despatched to collect it, possibly accompanied by one of the Guns if it is thought that the grouse might be able to get on the wing again. Otherwise, you simply work your dogs until all the shot birds are collected, then drop back with the rest of the shooting party while the other dog handler gets his pointers or setters out and hunting again.

Loading is perhaps the most specialised and arguably the most responsible job on a driven grouse shoot with the exception of that of the head keeper. It is not that the job is particularly difficult per se since opening a gun and replacing the spent cartridges with live rounds is a simple task, particularly when the gun is an ejector (as it will almost certainly be) and gets rid of the fired cases for you. The problem is that the loader, the Gun and possibly an interested spectator plus a dog or two are confined within the very limited space of a grouse butt; a grouse butt moreover that is likely to be built of stone. A shotgun is a surprisingly delicate article and it is all too easy to put an expensive dent into the barrels by knocking them against the sides of the butt or by dinging them against the barrels of the other gun while switching over.

The loader checks that the barrels are clear before the drive gets under way.

Gun and loader enjoying a chat as they wait for the first grouse to start coming through the line.

Bear in mind that a pair of best English guns will cost anything up to £100,000 – yes, that is one hundred thousand pounds – and you will see why a loader who puts a dent into a barrel or scratches a stock is unlikely to be popular. There is also the matter of safety to consider. When grouse are coming at speed and in numbers there has to be some smart choreography between Gun and loader as the Gun swings round to take a bird behind, then turns back to the front to pick up the next covey. The loader has to ensure that he is not in the way, both from the point of view of not interfering with the Gun's freedom to swing onto the grouse and also ensuring that he doesn't get into the line of fire.

The basics of loading are easy enough to grasp. The Gun fires one or both barrels from gun number 1 and then passes it to the loader holding it by the part of the stock immediately behind the trigger guard (the hand) in his right hand. The loader takes the fired gun in his left hand, grasping it by the fore end and puts the fore end of the loaded gun into the Gun's left hand. The loader then turns so that the muzzles are pointing in a safe direction, opens the fired gun and reloads it. It is up to the loader to ensure that the loaded gun is placed properly into the Gun's hand, since the Gun should be looking forward to spot the next target rather than looking at the loader. Done well this exchange of guns looks smooth and simple, but doing it well requires a certain amount of practice and a cool head from both parties.

The loader needs to have a supply of cartridges ready to hand for when the action gets hectic. When coveys of grouse are pouring over the butts in an unbroken mass it is not the time to be fumbling in a pocket for cartridges or struggling to free them from a cartridge belt. There are various designs of quick-release cartridge holders on the market – belts with snap-out clips, bags with extra-wide mouths and so on – but often the quickest and easiest way to ensure access to a ready supply of cartridges is to lay them out on top of the butt before the drive begins. Set them out neatly, all pointing in the same direction, and make sure that you won't be impeding the Gun when you reach for them. Some loaders carry a couple of cartridges between the fingers of their left hand ready to drop into the chambers as soon as the ejectors have flicked the fired rounds clear and this can certainly speed up loading by a fraction of a second or two provided that they have practised the technique beforehand.

Both loader and Gun should endeavour to stay calm no matter how many grouse are whistling through the line. Trying to rush, snatching at the changeover and grabbing for cartridges is more likely to slow things down than to speed them up and there is always the risk of a dented barrel or a finger getting nipped in the breech of a gun.

The loader may be able to help with keeping a note of how many birds are down and where they have fallen when the action is relatively slow, but that is not his main function. When guns need to be loaded and exchanged quickly it is not a good idea for the loader to be watching to see where shot birds are falling: his full concentration should be on the job of replacing fired cartridges and changing guns smoothly and safely.

Labrador racing back to its handler with a grouse.

Some Guns like to be warned when a covey is approaching the butts; others prefer that the loader leaves that responsibility to them. Some Guns welcome a string of ballistic advice from their loader; others much prefer that they are not told to give more lead, take them further out, let them come closer, etc. Some Guns like to indulge in general chat while waiting for the action to start: others prefer to be left alone to concentrate. Some Guns will appreciate that story about the camel, the harem girl and the sheikh; others prefer not to be distracted. It is up to the loader to try and sense what the Gun wants from him in the general areas of advice, instruction and conversation and then to try and abide by his preferences. If nothing else such sensitivity may be reflected in the size of the tip offered at the end of the day.

One area where the loader should not be afraid to make his presence felt is where safety is concerned. The cardinal sin for any Gun on a driven grouse shoot is to swing through the line. It is common for there to be some sort of physical device incorporated in the butt to prevent this happening – usually a couple of sticks that, in theory, should stop the Gun from continuing his swing through the line of butts. In practice, no matter what safety measures are taken, a really determined Gun can still end up with his muzzles pointing directly at the Gun in the next butt. He may not even be aware that he is doing it. Part of the loader's job is to ensure – as tactfully as possible – that this doesn't happen.

How this is achieved will depend on the individual character of both the loader and the Gun. A gentle suggestion that perhaps the last shot was a tad close to the neighbouring butt; an ostentatious repositioning of the sticks that are supposed to

Part of the loader's job is to clean the guns at the end of the shoot.

Picking-up with a keen and eager springer spaniel.

prevent the Gun from swinging through the line; physically preventing the Gun from being swung any closer to the danger area or perhaps uttering a few expletives… What will work with one Gun might go right over the head of another. Bear in mind that accusing a man of firing a dangerous shot is akin to accusing him of wife-beating in some quarters, but also bear in mind that if someone is shot and seriously injured and you might have been able to prevent it but did nothing, you will have to live with that knowledge for the rest of your life.

Always try to ensure that you have more than enough cartridges. Once the drive starts it will probably be virtually impossible for you to replenish your stocks if you have not taken sufficient into the butt to begin with. You will not be popular if your Gun is forced to stand and watch covey after covey sailing past his butt while the rest of his cartridges are sitting in a vehicle half a mile down the track. Take plenty: you will certainly not get into trouble for having cartridges left at the end of the drive.

Beating, picking-up, loading and flanking are all vital ingredients on a driven grouse shoot, but to many people taking part in a grouse shoot means shooting grouse. If you are fortunate enough to have been born into a family that owns a grouse moor then grouse shooting may well be a normal part of life. If you have friends who own grouse moors you may be invited to shoot grouse as a matter of course. If you are a single man and can contrive to marry someone whose family owns a grouse moor you may gain access to unlimited grouse shooting as well as gaining a wife. And vice versa if you are a single woman. In any of the above cases you are a lucky man – or woman – and I hope you appreciate just how fortunate you are. The rest of us have to resort to more commercial means to find some grouse shooting.

In general it is not difficult to go grouse shooting provided that you are prepared to pay the asking price. There are plenty of estates, sporting agents, hotels and moor owners who will sell you a day or a week or a month on a grouse moor or even the grouse moor itself if your pockets are deep enough. Magazines such as the *Shooting Times*, *The Field* and the *Shooting Gazette* carry advertisements from landowners and sporting agents with shooting to let and if you enter 'grouse shooting to let' or something similar into an internet search engine you will get several thousand hits a few of which may actually be of some use.

Obviously, in a good year grouse shooting will be easier to find than in a year when bad weather or disease has decimated stocks. You will also find a lot more choice if you want to shoot ten brace over dogs or spend a day walking up than if you want to arrange for a full team of Guns to shoot several hundred brace, but whatever you want – within reason – should be available somewhere provided that you are prepared to pay the asking price.

As to what the asking price is likely to be, at the time of writing walked up grouse shooting is available for about £70/£80 per brace with driven grouse costing around twice as much at £120/£140 per brace. The actual price will depend to some extent on what is on offer. The cost of walking up with your own dog over a bit of rough moorland where you might or might not stumble across the odd covey will be considerably cheaper than being taken out on a decent moor with a professional dog handler and a

The best way to take part is to shoot – ready for action with a pair of guns.

The gallery at a Pointer and Setter Trial enjoying a day on the moors and some first class dog work.

team of top quality birddogs where a bag of ten or twenty brace is practically guaranteed, assuming only that you can shoot straight. A driven day will never be cheap, but you would rightly expect to pay a lot more for the sort of shoot where you stay in the owner's stately home or castle overnight, are fed and watered as part of the package, have a loader supplied and generally get first class treatment all round than for shooting the same number of grouse on a moor where you simply turn up in the morning, supply your own packed lunch and make your own arrangements for accommodation.

You might well decide that the latter option offers a better return for your money since the same outlay would probably buy you a bit more shooting, or you may opt for the all round experience of a day or two spent in unaccustomed luxury – if such luxury is unaccustomed in your particular case. Another way of obtaining grouse shooting and some other sport besides is to hire a whole estate for a week or two. This is particularly common in Scotland where a Highland estate will probably offer deer stalking, salmon fishing and trout fishing as well as grouse shooting.

Quite a few estates in Scotland can be rented by the week and will include a lodge to stay in, perhaps the services of a cook, a caretaker to look after fires, boilers, boats and outboards and the like, a stalker or two to organise the sport and the chance to fish, shoot, stalk and generally live the life of a Highland laird for a week or two.

Sporting lets of this type can represent very good value for money – a lodge sleeping twelve people with salmon and trout fishing, stalking and the possibility of shooting grouse over pointers will cost from £3,000 per week upwards, depending on the quality of the sport on offer and the time of the year. August and September are the prime months for sport when grouse, stags and salmon are all in season, and lodges will be harder to find and more expensive to rent at those times. Even so, if you can put together a party of half a dozen couples who enjoy the whole Highland experience such a holiday can cost as little as £250 per head – plus food, drink, tips and travel expenses.

Some estates quote an all-in price while others charge a basic rent for the lodge and then add on a bit extra for each grouse shot or stag stalked. If no cook is supplied as part of the package there are a number of sporting cooks who specialise in catering for sporting tenants and are used to coping with the sometimes eccentric kitchen arrangements found in the more remote parts of the Highlands. There will usually be estate rifles available for would-be stalkers who don't have their own weapons and often fishing rods can be borrowed or hired if required. A week or two in a Highland lodge, fishing, stalking, shooting and walking, enjoying hearty breakfasts, picnic lunches and some good old-fashioned cooking in the evenings; peat fires and Victorian plumbing and no worries about driving home after a sniff of the cork at dinner is like sampling life in the golden age of sport. There are the midges though....

Two Labradors and a springer spaniel eager to be get into the action.

Picking-up team sweeping around the butts after the drive is over.

Every year organisations such as the Heather Trust organise fund-raising auctions where supporters donate a variety of lots that are auctioned off to the highest bidder and often include grouse shooting along with stalking, fishing, other forms of shooting, books, pictures and all sorts of other desirable things. There are usually guide prices to suggest how high the successful bidder is likely to have to go, though the better lots may well go for considerably more. Equally, some real bargains may be found particularly if you enquire as to which lots remain unsold after the closing date for bids.

Another way to get a flavour of the moors, grouse and the way that they were hunted back in Victorian times is to go along and watch a Pointer and Setter Field Trial. The main grouse trials begin about the middle of July and are run from then until the start of the shooting season on various estates in England and Scotland. No grouse are shot during the trials since the trials mostly take place before the shooting season begins, but they present a fascinating insight into the work of pointers and setters as well as giving the competitors and spectators the chance to get out onto some of the most exclusive estates in the country and savour the sights, sounds and smells of the grouse moor.

There are a number of societies that organise the individual trials but all are run under the auspices of the Kennel Club who can supply the aspiring spectator with details of where and when they are taking place. If you plan to go along and watch then a decent pair of boots and a waterproof coat are advisable, though with luck sunburn may be a bigger worry than keeping dry. The general course of the trial circuit is to begin in the north of England in mid-July and move to Scotland about the beginning of August working gradually northwards and finishing a day or two before shooting starts on the Twelfth of August. There is also a trial circuit in Ireland and details of those events can be obtained from the Irish Kennel Club.

If you are fortunate enough to live near a grouse moor, in northern England, Scotland, Ireland or Wales then it may be simplicity itself to get involved as a beater or, if you have a decent dog, a picker-up. For those who live in a city in the south of England taking part will involve a certain amount of effort and possibly the expenditure of a certain amount of money especially if you want to shoot grouse rather than help someone else to shoot them. If you really want to get involved and are prepared to expend the time and the effort and undertake the travel required you can find a way to get out onto the moors and play your part in the sport. And if driving two or three hundred miles to get to the nearest heather moorland seems like too much of an effort, just think back to the Victorian sportsman and the obstacles that had to be overcome in those days in order to travel to the same moor: by stagecoach, by sailing boat, on horseback or even on his own two feet. Taking part may not be easy, but for anyone who really wants to do so it should be possible. If you take part as a beater or a loader etc. you will probably be able to show a profit on the day.

Prospects for the Future

aking predictions is a dangerous business, particularly when they are set down on paper and will remain as a record of one's prescience or, more likely, of one's lack of it. Trying to second guess what will happen to grouse and grouse moors over the next few years doesn't seem too difficult at first sight – there are ample records of past years that can be extrapolated to produce a forecast of grouse prospects – but the procedure is complicated by the fact that the future of the red grouse cannot be viewed in isolation. There are too many other variables that may impact on that future and the two areas where that impact is likely to be felt most keenly are global warming and legislation.

No shortage of grouse to be collected at the end of this drive.

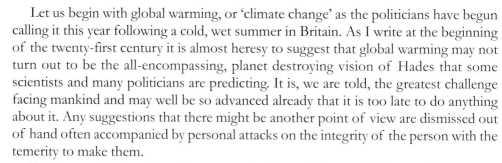

Let us begin with global warming, or 'climate change' as the politicians have begun calling it this year following a cold, wet summer in Britain. As I write at the beginning of the twenty-first century it is almost heresy to suggest that global warming may not turn out to be the all-encompassing, planet destroying vision of Hades that some scientists and many politicians are predicting. It is, we are told, the greatest challenge facing mankind and may well be so advanced already that it is too late to do anything about it. Any suggestions that there might be another point of view are dismissed out of hand often accompanied by personal attacks on the integrity of the person with the temerity to make them.

Forgive me if I tend to listen to such doom-laden predictions with a certain cynicism, but over the past fifty years or so I have been told on too many previous occasions that the end of life on earth as we know it is just around the corner. We were informed that the world's oil reserves would be totally exhausted before the end of the twentieth century; that a nuclear holocaust was inevitable; that fifty per cent of the UK population would contract HIV/AIDS within ten years; that cases of new variant CJD would sweep the country infecting anyone who had ever eaten a beef-burger; that the hole in the ozone layer spelt death to everyone who went out in the midday sun; that the next ice age was just around the corner; that acid rain was killing all the trees and that avian influenza would sweep the globe killing thousands upon thousands of people... So far none of those predictions has come true. I grant you that climate change/global warming may prove to be the exception but just for the moment I prefer to listen to the harbingers of doom with a fairly large pinch of salt.

That said, I am fully in favour of cutting down as much as possible on the levels of pollution that we spew into the atmosphere or drain into our rivers and oceans. I detest waste, whether it manifests as superfluous packaging at the supermarket, so-called 'mountains' of grain, butter, cheese and the like being produced, stored and then destroyed in the interests of the European Superstate or commercial shoots incinerating pheasants because there is no market readily available for their meat. But I do object to being told that I must happily embrace yet another new tax because it is 'green' or 'environmentally friendly'. Global warming/climate change seems at times to be the perfect excuse for governments to dip ever deeper into our pockets while assuring us that it is all for our own good. While scientists are receiving grants and bursaries to investigate climate change and governments can justify higher and higher levels of taxation in order to 'save' the planet I can confidently predict that global warming/climate change will stay at the forefront of their thoughts. At least until it all turns out to have been caused by increased sunspot activity whereupon something new and equally lucrative will come along to take its place.

And if, in fifty years' time, Edinburgh and Glasgow are just small clearings in the midst of a tropical rain forest then I will happily accept that I was wrong and the scientists and politicians were right. Except that one thing I can predict with absolute confidence is that in fifty year' time I will no longer be available to anyone who wants to say 'I told you so'.

Guns and beaters take a break for a chat between drives.

But assuming that there is some element of truth in the global warming argument, and that Britain will actually get warmer as a result (though some of the experts maintain that we will actually get colder as melting ice diverts the Gulf stream) then there are likely to be a number of consequences for grouse and grouse moors.

Loss of heather caused by heather beetle is likely to get worse if those who think that the best defence against the beetle is a long, cold winter with frosts that bite deep into the ground and kill off the beetles and their larvae are correct. Likewise, the apparent increase in tick-borne diseases such as louping ill and of grouse chicks being killed by the sheer burden of these parasites is likely to continue since there is also evidence that tick numbers are cut back during cold weather. Unless the rise in temperatures is really dramatic I doubt whether being a degree or so warmer will have any effect on the range over which the grouse can thrive. They were once found on the mainland from Dartmoor to Caithness and there has always been a marked difference in mean temperatures between one end of the country and the other suggesting that grouse are tolerant of reasonably wide variations in summer and winter climate.

Taking a shot behind the line watched by dogs and loader.

Rising sea levels, which are also supposed to happen as a result of climate change, are unlikely to have much effect on grouse given the elevation of most heather moorland. Certainly if the habitat of the red grouse, let alone the ptarmigan, is ever in danger of inundation from tidal waters grouse shooting is likely to be the last thing on the minds of the majority of Britain's population.

Provided that moorland owners and keepers are able to maintain viable populations of grouse it seems likely that there will be little further loss of heather habitat to other commercial interests such as farming and forestry. The days of big grants encouraging landowners to plant trees or convert moorland into grassland are over for the time being and unlikely to return in the foreseeable future. Grouse – where there are grouse – are a more valuable commodity than timber or mutton and simple economics would suggest that they will take precedence over other forms of land management. There may even be a slight increase in the total acreage of heather moorland as owners try to recover areas that have been lost to farming and forestry in past years.

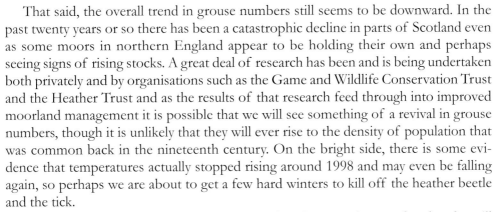

That said, the overall trend in grouse numbers still seems to be downward. In the past twenty years or so there has been a catastrophic decline in parts of Scotland even as some moors in northern England appear to be holding their own and perhaps seeing signs of rising stocks. A great deal of research has been and is being undertaken both privately and by organisations such as the Game and Wildlife Conservation Trust and the Heather Trust and as the results of that research feed through into improved moorland management it is possible that we will see something of a revival in grouse numbers, though it is unlikely that they will ever rise to the density of population that was common back in the nineteenth century. On the bright side, there is some evidence that temperatures actually stopped rising around 1998 and may even be falling again, so perhaps we are about to get a few hard winters to kill off the heather beetle and the tick.

The other pressure likely to bear on grouse shooting over the next few decades will come from legislation. The government has already tried to ban hunting and coursing and there are clear indications that shooting is under threat as well. Pressure groups of different kinds varying from those who simply oppose any form of blood sport on principle to those who have other agendas that clash with the best interests of the grouse all seek to claim the attention of politicians and further their own causes. Although there are sound economic arguments for preserving and encouraging grouse shooting and obvious environmental benefits from proper moorland management there is no guarantee that common sense will prevail once our legislators are persuaded to take action.

The threat to the rural economy, mass rallies attended by hundreds of thousands of protestors, the potential loss of thousands of jobs, the destruction of a whole way of life and the likely death of several thousand hounds had no effect whatsoever on the minds of the politicians in Scotland and England who voted to ban hunting with dogs. It is true that the laws they actually passed were so incompetently drafted that hunting is continuing in some form despite their efforts, but the point remains that logic and sense play little part in the thinking of a politician when class hatred and pig ignorance are the main driving forces. (And I apologise to any pigs that quite reasonably resent being classed alongside certain of our elected representatives.) So the fact that banning shooting in general and grouse shooting in particular would be detrimental to the countryside in a whole raft of different ways is by no means an insurance against it happening.

There are several possible ways in which grouse shooting might be threatened. An outright ban on shooting for sport seems unlikely but there is no telling what a future left-wing government might do given a big enough majority and sufficient cash donations from anti-fieldsports organisations. It seems more likely that there will be legislation passed that limits the ability of keepers to control predators – a ban on the use of snares and tunnel traps perhaps – or that restricts the use of the lamp and rifle as a fox control measure. The latter might well occur through the efforts of the Health and Safety movement that seems to be casting an increasingly restrictive net around practically everything, often with ludicrous consequences. When Community Support Officers (a sort of substitute for proper policemen) stand by and watch a child drown because they are not allowed to attempt a rescue for health and safety reasons, or paramedics are not allowed to run to an emergency in case they trip up and injure themselves then it is not hard to imagine what the attitude of H&S would be towards firing a powerful rifle across open moorland at night.

Increased access to the countryside has not yet had the damaging effect on grouse shooting that some landowners feared. To some extent this is because they are allowed to restrict access to moorland by the public at nesting time and on shooting days but there is no guarantee that this balance will not be disturbed by some future legislation. Heather burning is essential for the grouse but it is viewed with displeasure by those who would like to see much of our open moorland revert to woodland. There are arguments that can be made in favour of this though they would find little sympathy from those with the interests of the grouse at heart, but once again, there is no certainty that parliament will listen to one side of the debate rather than another despite the vested interests of the moorland owners.

Indirectly, ever tighter controls on the legal ownership of guns and rifles may have a long term impact on the number of people who take up shooting as a hobby or who find employment in one of the related professions. I would expect shotgun ownership to be subjected to the same tight restrictions that apply to rifles within a few years. Then anyone wanting to own a shotgun will have to provide 'good reason' for having it rather than simply having to satisfy the police that there is no reason why they should not be granted a certificate. No doubt they will be required to be a member of a clay pigeon shooting club, or have to show proof that they have somewhere to use the gun for game shooting or pest control. Of themselves such measures will simply be a bit more red tape to be negotiated each time a shotgun certificate is renewed, but they will also provide a considerable disincentive for newcomers to the sport. It is unlikely that they will have any effect whatsoever on the growing levels of gun crime, since criminals, by and large, tend not to apply for certification for their pistols and sawn-off shotguns.

Overall I think the prospects for grouse and grouse shooting are quite bright in England, but rather more mixed in Scotland where some areas are still producing respectable bags while others, particularly in the far north, are struggling to prevent the grouse from disappearing altogether. In Wales and Ireland, apart from isolated pockets it is hard to see the red grouse ever returning to the population levels that would see it back as a major quarry species and with such a poor outlook it is hard to see where the necessary investment might come from to try and achieve this.

It would probably be over optimistic to suggest that the future looks completely rosy for the grouse in Britain but I do think that it looks quite bright in those areas where grouse shooting is important enough to make a real contribution to the local economy. In other areas, where the decline has been such that grouse shooting is little more than a peripheral activity, we are less likely to see the investment that may be

This Gun takes time for a quick rest before the next drive starts…

…and this Labrador seems to have the same idea in mind.

Counting the bag at the end of a superb day's driven grouse shooting.

needed to revive grouse stocks. It is hard to justify the outlay needed to employ a team of keepers with all their associated infrastructure when there may be no return in sporting terms for many years, if ever.

The best hope for such places is that the root cause – if there is a root cause – of the fall in grouse numbers is identified and found to be something that can be put right. Then the red grouse in Scotland, Wales and Ireland might once again flourish in the sort of numbers that drew sportsmen to the wildest regions of those countries despite all the difficulties and discomforts involved with travel and accommodation in the early years of the nineteenth century or the colossal expense of owning and managing a grouse moor during the twentieth. Sadly, I am not convinced that it will ever happen. Hopefully future years will prove me wrong.

Useful Addresses

Two of the main organisations concerned with the preservation, improvement, promotion and management of heather moorland are the Heather Trust and the Moorland Association. Details of both are listed below as detailed on their web sites, along with some of the other organisations that may be of interest to land owners, keepers, moorland managers and anyone else who finds Britain's heather moorlands a magical place to work, play and simply to enjoy.

The Heather Trust

The Heather Trust is a charity dedicated to the promotion of high standards of moorland management. The Trust seeks to improve moorland habitat for the benefit of wildlife, domestic stock, game and all people with an interest in moorland areas.

Address: The Heather Trust, Newtonrigg, Holywood, Dumfries, Scotland, DG2 0RA. Telephone 01387 723201. Website Heathertrust.co.uk

The Moorland Association

Was set up to encourage public understanding about heather moorland and to advise government and moor owners on moorland management and to represent the owners in negotiations with government, nature conservation and other bodies.

Address: The Moorland Association, 16 Castle Park, Lancaster, LA1 1YG. Telephone 01524 846846. Website Moorlandassociation.org

The Countryside Alliance

The Countryside Alliance is the primary focus for the defence of all fieldsports against those who threaten them on political or moral grounds.

Address: The Countryside Alliance, The Old Town Hall, 367 Kennington Road, London, SE11 4PT. Telephone 0207 840 9274. Website www.countryside-alliance.com.

British Association for Shooting and Conservation (BASC)

BASC was formed from the old Wildfowlers Association of Great Britain and Ireland (WAGBI). It campaigns against political interference in shooting and also runs conservation and research programmes as well as providing third-party insurance for its members.

Address: BASC, Marford Mill, Rossett, Wrexham, Clywd, LL12 0HL. Telephone 01244 573000. Website www.basc.org.uk

Game and Wildlife Conservation Trust

This is a charitable trust and thus precluded from the political campaigning that the other shooting organisations carry out. It is deeply involved in research into all aspects of game and countryside management and conservation and provides a valuable advisory service to its members.

Address: Game and Wildlife Conservation Trust, Fordingbridge, Hampshire, SP6 1EF. Telephone 01425 652381. Website www.gct.org.uk

The National Gamekeepers Organisation (NGO)

The NGO promotes the work of gamekeepers, supports and defends the work of both professional and amateur keepers and campaigns on behalf of shooting and fieldsports in general.

Address: NGO, PO Box 107, Bishop Auckland, DL14 9YW. Telephone 01388 718502. Website www.nationalgamekeepers.org.uk

The Scottish Gamekeepers Association (SGA)

The SGA is the Scottish equivalent of the NGO.

Address: The Scottish Gamekeepers Association, PO Box 7477, Perth, Perthshire, PH2 7YE. Telephone 01738 587515. Website www.scottishgamekeepers.co.uk

The Kennel Club

The Kennel Club, 1-5 Clarges Street, Picadilly, London, W1J 8AB. Telephone 0870 606 6750. Website The-Kennel-Club.org.uk

The Irish Kennel Club

The Irish Kennel Club, Fottrell House, Harolds X Bridge, Dublin 6W, Ireland. Telephone +353 (1) 4533300. Website www.ikc.ie

Index